# LUTHERAN CHURCH BASEMENT WOMEN

# LUTHERAN
# CHURCH
# BASEMENT  WOMEN

BY
JANET LETNES MARTIN
and ALLEN TODNEM

Illustrated by
ALLEN TODNEM

REDBIRD  PRODUCTIONS
BOX  363
HASTINGS,  MN   55033

THIS BOOK IS DEDICATED
TO LUTHERAN CHURCH BASEMENT WOMEN.

# LUTHERAN CHURCH BASEMENT WOMEN
## Table of Contents

# LUTHERAN SONG, POEM & PRAYER

Verse 1

The first words one hears when the tel-e-phone rings So sorry to hear that Now what can I bring. The food that is brought in is fit for a King The humble re-ply is 'Oh dats ing-a-ting. OH — us Lutheran church wo-men we're none but the best. We come in to serve from the east or the west. The basements' our home we will work night or day. We clean and we cook the old fashioned way ——

Verse 2

Sometimes it is pickles, hotdish or a cake
often the call it comes in very late
with no time to spare a dish one must bake
It's always from scratch Now make no mistake!

Verse 3

A funeral, a shower Oh what will it be -
You come to church early and no one you see
The kitchen's a mess, the League had the key
Oh Lord I do ask you, is it all up to me?

2

# LUTHERAN CHURCH BASEMENT WOMEN

Verse 1

The  first words one hears when the telephone rings,
so sorry to hear that, now what can I bring.
The food that is brought in is fit for a king,
the humble reply is oh dats ing-a-ting.

Verse 2

Sometimes it is pickles, hotdish or a cake,
often the call it comes in very late.
With no time to spare, a dish one must bake,
It's always from scratch, now make no mistake!

Verse 3

A funeral, a shower, oh what will it be,
you come to church early and no one you see.
The kitchen's a mess, the league had the key,
oh Lord I do ask you, is it all up to me?

Refrain:

OH-Us Lutheran church women we're none but the best,
we come into serve from the east or the west.
The basement's our home, we will work night or day,
we'll clean and we cook the old fashioned way.

## THE LADIES' AID

The old church bell had long been cracked; its call was but a groan,
It seemed to sound a funeral knell with every broken tone.
"We need a bell", the brethren said, "but taxes must be paid.
We have no money we can spare.  Just ask the Ladies' Aid."

The shingles on the roof were old; the rain came down in rills,
The brethren slowly shook their heads and read the monthly bills.
The chairman of the board arose and said, "I am afraid
That we shall have to lay the case before the Ladies' Aid."

The preacher's salary was behind; the poor man blushed to meet
The grocer and the butcher when they passed him on the street.
But nobly spoke the brethren then, "Pastor, you shall be paid.
We'll call upon the treasurer of our good Ladies' Aid."

"Oh," said the man, "the way to heaven is long and hard and steep,
With slopes of ease on either side, the path is hard to keep.
We can not climb the heights alone; our hearts are sore dismayed!
We ne'er shall get to heaven at all without the Ladies' Aid."

4

## A KITCHEN PRAYER

Lord of all pots and pans and things,
since I've not time to be
A saint by doing lovely things
or watching late with Thee
Or dreaming in the dawn light
or storming Heaven's gates,
Make me a saint by getting meals
and washing up the plates.

Warm all the kitchen with Thy love,
and light it with Thy peace,
Forgive me all my worrying
and make my grumbling cease,
Thou who didst love to give men food,
in room or by the sea
Accept this service that I do,
I do it unto Thee.

# BEVERAGES

# LUTHERAN BEVERAGES

## COFFEE

### Watkins Coffee for Fifty

1 pound Watkins Ground Coffee    2 1/2 gallons boiling
3 eggs    water

Beat eggs, add coffee and mix well. Add enough cold water to blend. Tie mixture in cheesecloth bag, add boiling water and boil 5 minutes. Lower heat, add 1 cup cold water, let settle 10 minutes over low fire.

### EGG COFFEE

Bring to boil 6 to 7 cups water. Add 3 Tbsp. coffee which has been mixed with part of an egg. Boil coffee until the foam disappears being careful so it doesn't cook over. Fill the remainder of the pot with boiling water. To settle the grounds add a bit of cold water.

## COLD DRINKS

### LEMON NECTAR DRINK
*Delicious, Refreshing Drink*

2 tsp. Watkins Lemon    2 tsp. sugar, blend sugar
   Nectar Syrup    and syrup
2 tsp. sugar    2/3 glass iced water

Stir in mixture and add an ice cube.

### ORANGEADE

1/3 C. lemon juice    2 C. granulated sugar
1 C. orange juice (strain)    4 C. water
2 oranges, peel, remove seeds
   and slice

Boil sugar and water to a syrup. Let cook, add juice and ice water. Stir.

## WATKINS CHERRY NECTAR DRINK

| | |
|---|---|
| 1 to 2 tsp. Watkins Cherry nectar Syrup 3/4 glass cold water | 2 or more tsp. sugar to taste |

Add sugar to nectar syrup, mix well, add ice water, stir and serve.

## WATKINS FRUIT PUNCH

| | |
|---|---|
| 3/4 bottle Watkins Cherry Nectar 3/4 bottle Watkins Lemon Nectar | 1/2 bottle Orange Nectar 5 pounds sugar 5 gallons water, ice cold |

Blend Watkins Nectar Syrup and sugar and slowly stir in the water or a thin syrup may be made of the sugar and water. When cold, stir in the Watkins Nectar Syrup. Serve with ice cubes.

## QUICK AND EASY PUNCH

| | |
|---|---|
| 1 pkg. any flavored kool-aid 1 tray of ice cubes (12 cubes) | 1 C sugar |

Dissolve sugar and kool-aid in tap water. Stir well. Add ice. Serves 8.

For company add a lemon slice. For silver wedding anniversaries, add one quart ginger ale to above mixture.

# COCKTAILS

# COCKTAILS

## FANCY COCKTAILS

### TOMATO COCKTAIL JUICE

To make delicious tomato juice cocktail, add 1 tsp. Worcestershire Sauce, 1/8 tsp. celery salt, 1/8 tsp. pepper to each cup of tomato juice used. Mix, chill and serve.

### TOMATO JUICE COCKTAIL

3 C tomato juice
3 whole cloves
1 bay leaf
1 Tbsp minced onion
1 tsp spicy meat sauce

2 tsp sugar
3 Tbsp lemon juice
1/2 tsp salt (or less)
pepper

Simmer a short time, strain, chill and serve.

### EVERYDAY LUTHERAN COCKTAILS

Chill juice thoroughly. Serve in juice glasses while cold.

# BREADS

"She needeth least, who kneadeth best,
those rules which we shall tell. Who
kneadeth ill, shall need them more
than she who kneadeth well."

# BREADS

## WHITE BREAD

### 2 LOAVES

1 cake compressed yeast
  or 1 pkg. fast
2 Tbsp. sugar
6 to 6 1/2 C. sifted all
  purpose flour

granular yeast
2 C. liquid
1 Tbsp. salt
2 Tbsp. shortening
  (melted and cooled)

### 4 LOAVES

2 cakes compressed yeast
  Or 2 pkgs. fast
4 Tbsp. sugar
12 to 12 1/2 C. sifted all
  purpose flour

granular yeast
4 C. liquid
2 Tbsp. salt
4 Tbsp. shortening
  (melted and cooled)

### 6 LOAVES

2 cakes compressed yeast
  Or 2 pkgs. fast
6 Tbsp. sugar
18 to 18 1/2 C. sifted all
  purpose flour

granular yeast
6 C. liquid
3 Tbsp. salt
6 Tbsp. shortening
  (melted and cooled)

METHOD:
1. If using milk, measure, scald and partially cool. (Water or potato water does not need to be scalded.) Measure and melt shortening, allow to cool.
2. Crumble yeast into mixing bowl.
3. Add liquid at proper temperature.
4. Measure sugar and salt and stir them in. Let stand until thoroughly dissolved, about 5 minutes.
5. Sift and measure flour. Add 1/2 of it. Beat with spoon until smooth and very elastic. (Batter will fall from spoon in "sheets.")
6. Beat in melted and cooled shortening.
7. Add most of remaining flour and work it in with the hand (possibly using the maximum amount) until dough is possible to handle. Mix well.
8. Turn dough onto lightly floured board, cover, let stand 10 min. to tighten up, then knead until smooth and elastic.

17

9. Round up and set to rise again until not quite double in bulk, about 45 minutes.
10. Punch down dough.
11. Round up and set to rise again until not quite double in bulk, about 45 minutes.
12. Punch down dough. Divide for loaves. Round up each part, cover, and let rest 15 minutes.
13. Mold into loaves.
14. Put into greased bread loaf pans. The dough should fill pans 2/3 full. Cover with damp cloth, and let rise at proper temperature until sides of dough have reached top of pan and center is well rounded out above (1 1/2 to 2 hours). The dough should feel very light when touched gently with finger.
15. Bake 35 to 45 minutes in a hot oven (450 degrees) for the first 15 minutes then reduce heat to moderate oven (375 degrees) to finish baking. When baked, bread has a hollow sound when tapped and comes away from side of the pan.

## VARIATIONS FROM SAME DOUGH
(Measurements form 2 loaves)

Nut bread - add 2 cups coarsely chopped nuts.
Date bread - add 2 cups cut-up dates.
Raisin bread - add 2 cups raisins (either seeded or seedless).
Cracked wheat bread - add 4 Tbsp. honey and 2 cups cracked wheat.
Whole Wheat bread - add 8 Tbsp. molasses and 1 1/2 cups whole wheat or graham flour.
Swedish Rye - add 4 Tbsp. molasses, 4 Tbsp. dark corn syrup, and 1 1/2 cups rye flour. (Bake at 375 degrees - 400 degrees for 35 to 45 minutes).

A new Lutheran bride can't expect to make perfect Lutheran bread right away. Practice makes perfect and after some time a Lutheran woman doesn't even have to measure ingredients but goes by the fall of the bread.

## GRANDMA'S WATER RISING NUT TWISTS

2 pkgs. dry yeast dissolved in 1/4 cup warm water
1/2 C. shortening                 3 Tbsp. sugar

1/2 tsp. salt                          1 tsp. vanilla
1/3 C. scalded milk

Combine the five above ingredients, then add the yeast mixture.

1 1/2 C. flour blended in
3 eggs beaten in one at a time

Cover and let rise for 15 minutes.

1 1/2 C. flour blended in to above (3 C. flour in all)
    (The dough will be quite soft)

Grandma's way: Tie dough in soft cloth size of small dish towel
to allow dough to expand. Place in large bowl of warm water (75
to 80 degrees). Let stand to allow dough to rise to top of water -
(about 30 to 45 minutes). Remove from water, the dough will
be soft and moist.

My Way: Set bowl of dough in a warm place (80 to 90 degrees)
for about half an hour covered.

Coating:   1 C. chopped nuts, any kind
           3/4 cups sugar
           1 tsp. cinnamon

Stir this mixture on a large piece of waxed paper. Dip out
rounded tablespoon of soft dough, and roll in nut mixture, then
either make 3 or 4 inch long twist, pressing ends down on
greased cookie sheets, or tie this long strip into a loose knot and
place on cookie sheet (the latter keeps it shape better). Let stand
for 10 minutes. Bake in 375 degrees oven overbrowning on
bottom, then put a shallow pan or water or sheet of tinfoil on the
lower grid. This makes about 25 mouth watering delicacies, that
are convenient because they are served without butter.

History:  Grandma used to make these for her church lady
organizations. When her hands got too arthritic to be dextrous,
she supervised me until I could turn out a product almost as good
as hers. I have put down my modernizations here, but I still
make them for my husband to take to church men's coffee hours
when it is "his turn" .                          -Mrs. G. Gudmestad

## BANANA BREAD

| | |
|---|---|
| 1 C. sugar | 3 mashed bananas |
| 1/2 C. lard | 2 cups flour |
| 1 tsp. soda | 2 eggs |
| 3 Tbsp hot water | 1/4 tsp. salt |

Mix shortening, sugar and eggs well beaten. Dissolve soda in hot water, and add one cup flour. Then add bananas and second cup of flour. Bake at 375 degrees for 45 minutes.

*Do when bananas are 10 cents a pound. Stock up and bake like crazy. Freezes well. Handy to have on hand.*

### JULEKAKE (basic dough for any rolls)

| | |
|---|---|
| 5 1/2 C. flour | 1/4 C. shortening |
| 1 1/2 tsp. salt | 1/2 C. sugar |
| 1 1/2 C. milk | 2 cakes compressed yeast |
| 2 eggs | |

Scald milk and add sugar; cool to lukewarm. Add yeast cakes and let stand 5 minutes. Add 3 cups flour, beat, then add salt and eggs and beat again. Blend shortening in and add remaining flour. Knead well, put in oiled bowl to rise until double in bulk. Punch down and let rise again. Add currants, citron and candied fruit. Shape into round loaf pan, let rise and bake. Frost with powdered sugar icing.

*This makes more than 1 loaf, but we're not sure how many. This is made only at Christmas time in Lutheran circles. It is served only for festive events and not at funerals. It just wouldn't be appropriate.*

### LIGHT AND AIRY BUNS

| | |
|---|---|
| 1 C. lukewarm | 2 tsp. sugar |
| 2 pkg. dry yeast | 1/2 C. sugar |
| 1/2 C. shortening (melted) | |

| | |
|---|---|
| 3 small tsp. salt | 2 Tbsp. vinegar |
| 3 1/2 C. lukewarm water | 8 to 10 C. flour |

Combine water, sugar, and yeast. Let stand about 10 minutes. Into a large bowl put sugar, shortening, salt, vinegar, water, and flour. Knead real good and let rise twice. Pinch off dough about the size of a crab apple. Place on greased cookie sheets or cake pan. Let rise again. Bake 15 to 20 minutes at 400 degrees. Makes about 60 buns.

*These buns were always served when the new pastor moved into the parsonage. Make them big for funerals and open face them. Great for spam spread topping.*

## LIMPA
### (Swedish Rye Bread)

| | |
|---|---|
| 2 cakes compressed yeast | 1 C. sugar |
| 4 C. buttermilk | 3 Tbsp. salt |
| 1 tsp. soda | 1/2 C. molasses |
| 1 C. water | 6 C. rye flour |
| 1/2 C. shortening | 8 C. white flour |

METHOD: Dissolve yeast in 1/2 cup water, add 1 teaspoon sugar. Combine sugar, shortening, salt, molasses and water and bring to a boil. Add soda to buttermilk, then add hot liquid mixture. Add yeast when liquid is lukewarm. Add rye flour and beat thoroughly then add enough white flour to make a stiff dough. Knead well and place in greased bowl to rise until light; knead down once and when light shape into 6 round loaves. Place on greased tins and let rise until light, then bake at 375 degrees for about 45 minutes.

VARIATIONS: 2 cups of raisins may be added if desired. Honey may be used in place of sugar for sweetening. Grated rind of 3 oranges may be added for flavor.

*A favorite for Swedes, but Norwegians eat it, especially Norwegians that are Lutherans.*

## "MORS GROV BRØD"
### (Brown Bread)

1 cake compressed yeast
4 C. lukewarm water
1/2 C. molasses
2 Tbsp. salt
1/2 C. melted shortening

9 C. white flour
3 C. whole wheat or
   graham flour
1/2 C. sugar

METHOD: Dissolve yeast in 1/2 C. lukewarm water; let stand 15 minutes. Add 3 1/2 cups lukewarm water, molasses, salt, sugar and shortening. Add enough flour to make a soft dough. Beat thoroughly for about 10 minutes, then add the rest of flour to make stiff dough. Knead, then place in greased bowl, cover and set in warm place. When double in bulk, knead again. Let rise once more, then shape into loaves. Let rise until light, then bake about 45 minutes in moderate oven. Brush tops with melted butter. Makes 4 medium size loaves. For a delicious nut bread try adding chopped walnuts to part of dough. Bake as usual.

*Every Lutheran Grandma knows this recipe. As basic as the four food groups.*

## RYE BREAD

1 cake yeast, compressed
1/4 C. white sugar
1/8 C. brown sugar
2 C. warm water
3 or 4 Tbsp. molasses

1 egg
1 Tbsp. salt
4 1/2 C. white flour
2 1/2 C. rye flour
4 Tbsp. melted shortening

Crumble yeast in 1/4 cup warm water and let soften for five minutes. Dissolve sugar and salt in remaining warm water. Add dissolved yeast, beaten egg and molasses. Add rye flour, beat well. Add melted shortening and white flour gradually to make stiff dough. Turn onto a floured board and knead well. Place in greased bowl, cover and let rise in a warm place until double in bulk. Punch down, let rise again. Then knead and form into loaves. Place in oiled pans, cover and let rise until light. Bake 10 minutes at 425 degrees at 40 minutes at 375 degrees.

Swedish Rye and rye are not one and the same. Promoters of Norwegian Lutheran lutefisk suppers sometimes feature Swedish Rye to get ticket sales up.

## SWEDISH TEA RING

| | |
|---|---|
| 2 cakes compressed yeast | 1/2 C. sugar |
| 1/4 C. lukewarm water | 1 tsp. salt |
| 1 C. milk | 2 eggs, beaten |
| 1/4 C. butter | 5 C. flour |

Soften yeast in lukewarm water. Scald milk. Add butter, sugar and salt. Cool to lukewarm. Add flour to make a thick batter. Add yeast and eggs. Beat well. Add enough flour to make a soft dough. Turn out on lightly floured board and knead until satiny. Place in greased bowl, cover and let rise until double in bulk (about two hours). When light, punch down, shape into tea ring, rolls or coffee cakes. Let rise until double in bulk (half to three-quarters hour). Bake at 375 degrees for twenty-five to thirty minutes for coffee cakes, twenty to twenty-five minutes for rolls. This recipe makes 2 12-inch tea rings or 3 dozen rolls.

*Some Swedes really out do themselves and gussy this tea ring up with Maraschino Cherries.*

## THREE-DAY BUNS

| | |
|---|---|
| 5 C. boiling water | 1 cake compressed yeast |
| 2 Tbsp. sugar | 1/4 C. lukewarm water |
| 1 tsp. salt | 6 C. flour |
| 4 Tbsp. melted butter | |

Dissolve yeast in the lukewarm water. Pour boiling water over sugar and butter. When cool, add salt, yeast and flour to make stiff dough. Set dough in ice box. Let rise twice and knead down. Let rise again. Form into buns and place on oiled pans. Let stand over night. Bake in the morning.

*If you have the time these are good. Lutheran Women whose husbands are retired have time to make these. Some retired Lutheran husbands even watch them bake. This recipe makes 3 dozen large buns. Bake for 20 minutes at 375 degrees.*

## WHITE BREAD

| | |
|---|---|
| 11 3/4 C. bread flour | 2 1/4 C. water |
| 2 C. milk | 1/4 C. sugar |
| 1 1/2 cakes yeast (compressed | 4 tsp. salt |
| or granular) | 2 Tbsp. shortening |

Crumble the yeast into a quarter cup of lukewarm water, and let it soften for five minutes. Scald the milk. Add sugar, salt and cold water. Stir thoroughly until salt and sugar are dissolved. Pour into a large mixing bowl. Allow milk to cool until lukewarm. Pour softened yeast into the lukewarm milk mixture. Stir until well mixed. No chunks of yeast should remain separate after stirring. Add half of the sifted flour to the milk mixture. Stir the dough until flour and liquids are thoroughly mixed into a batter. (Note: Adding half of the flour at this time prevents streaks in the bread and helps to make a moist loaf which will keep fresh longer.) Melt the shortening. Allow to cool and add to the batter and stir thoroughly. Add the remaining sifted flour and mix well. Stir flour into batter until batter takes up the flour. After letting dough rest on floured board for ten minutes, knead dough twelve minutes. Place dough in lightly greased bowl, and allow to rise in a warm place approximately two and one-half hours. Punch down and form into loaves. Allow to rise until double in bulk and bake. Bake this bread for 50 minutes at 400 degrees.

*This recipe makes 4 loaves and is similar to another one in this book. If the other one doesn't work out use this one.*

## WHOLE WHEAT BREAD

| | |
|---|---|
| 2 eggs | 2 C. graham or whole |
| 1 C. brown sugar | wheat flour |
| 2 1/2 C. rich sour milk or | 2 tsp. baking powder |
| buttermilk | 1/2 tsp. salt |
| 2 tsp. soda | 1 C. raisins (ground) |
| 2 C. white flour | |

Beat eggs. Add milk and sugar. Add the sifted dry ingredients. Mix thoroughly. Add raisins. Place in an oiled pan to bake at 325 degrees for 1 hour. This makes 2 9 x 5 loaves.

*This is hearty bread. Egg salad is good on this bread at home. Peanut butter and banana on whole wheat is a good treat but never served in a Lutheran Church. (These breads in this chapter are arranged alphabetically).*

# PASS THE PICKLES PLEASE

# "PASS THE PICKLES PLEASE"

## BEET PICKLES

Cook beets until tender. Slip skins and slice if beets are large. Place in clean hot jars, cover with boiling syrup and seal.

SYRUP:
1 C sugar

1 pint vinegar
few whole cloves

*These add color to any table spread.*

## BREAD AND BUTTER PICKLES

1 gallon cucumbers
2 green peppers

8 small white onions
1/2 C. salt

Select fresh, crisp cucumbers of dill pickling size. Wash but do not peel. Slice crosswise in paper thin slices. Slice onions thin and shred peppers thin. Mix salt with the vegetables and bury pieces of cracked ice in the mixture. Cover with weighted plate and let stand three hours. Drain thoroughly. In the meantime, make syrup as follows:

5 C. sugar
5 C. vinegar
2 Tbsp. mustard seed

1/2 tsp. ground cloves
1 tsp. celery seed
1 1/2 tsp. turmeric

Mix sugar, turmeric and cloves; add mustard, celery seeds and vinegar. Mix well and pour over pickles. Put on low heat and heat to scalding but do not boil. Lift mixture occasionally with paddle while heating. Seal in hot, sterilized jars.

*These go well with funeral meals.*

## CHUNK PICKLES

Wash cucumbers and put in brine whole (Brine is water with salt in enough to float an egg). Soak in brine 3 days. On the 4th day drain off brine water and soak in clear water. On the 5th day cut cucumbers in chunks an put them in a weakened vinegar solution and 1 T. alum. Simmer for 2 hours. Also add green food coloring. After 2 hours drain off water and make brine of 2 cups vinegar, 2 quarts sugar and spices in a bag which consists of 1 oz. stick cinnamon, 1 oz. whole cloves, 1 oz. whole allspice. After it comes to a boil, pour it over the pickles. This is enough brine for a dishpan of pickles. For at least 3 mornings after that, drain off brine and add 1 cup sugar and 1 cup vinegar. After 3rd day put in jars and seal.

*These pickles go very good with minced ham spread on buns.*

## CRAB APPLE PICKLES

Remove flower end of apple and replace with a clove. To 5 pounds of apples use 3 3/4 pounds of sugar and a 5 cent box of stick cinnamon. (It cost a little more now.).

Place layer of apples in 1 gallon jar, then a layer of sugar and broken sticks of cinnamon. When jar is full, pour over it 1 quart vinegar. Put cover on jar and bake slowly 2 hours. When cool place paraffin and paper over top and put away. Use stone jar.

## CUCUMBER PICKLES
### *Watkins Mixed Spices*

Slice large cucumbers, cover with salted water overnight. Fill 2 quart jars with cucumbers. Add 2 teaspoons Watkins Mustard, 2 teaspoons sugar, 1 teaspoon Watkins Mixed Spices, 1 teaspoon celery seed. Fill jar with hot vinegar and seal in sterilized jars.

## CUCUMBER PICKLES

| | |
|---|---|
| 2 oz. white mustard seed | 1 peck cucumbers |
| 2 oz. black mustard seed | 1/2 qt. small onions |
| 2 oz juniper berries | 2 lbs sugar |
| 2 oz celery seed | 1/2 dz. small green peppers |

1 gallon vinegar                    Watkins Mixed Spices

Put 1 peck inch-long cucumbers in salt and water, cover tightly, let stand 3 days. Put seeds in bags and boil 15 minutes in 1 gallon vinegar. Add small piece alum and pour hot over cucumbers which have been removed from water. When cool, heat again several times until ready for use.

## CUCUMBER RELISH

| | |
|---|---|
| 1 qt. cucumbers | 3 tsp. celery seed |
| 1 qt. onions | 3 Tbsp Watkins Dry |
| 1 qt. cabbage | Mustard |
| 3 red peppers (sweet) | 3 tsp. turmeric |
| 1 qt. vinegar | Salt to taste |
| 4 C. light brown sugar | Watkins Mixed Spices |
| 1/2 C. flour | |

Peel and chop cucumbers, remove seeds (after being chopped, then measure). Put all together, boil 15 minutes.

## SYLTELABBER
### *(Pickled Pig's Feet)*

Clean and scrape pig's feet thoroughly; cut in halves lengthwise and cook in salted water until tender. Cook vinegar enough to cover with 1/2 C. sugar to 3 cups vinegar and 1 cup water. Add pepper, whole all-spice and few whole cloves for seasoning. Pour this solution boiling hot over the prepared pig's feet. When cold, place in refrigerator until ready to use. Let stand 2 days before using.

*A real treat at Christmas.*

## STRING BEAN PICKLES

| | |
|---|---|
| 1 peck string beans | 3 pints vinegar |
| 3 lbs sugar | 3 lbs sugar |
| 1 C. flour | 2 Tbsp. dry mustard |
| 2 Tbsp celery seed | 2 Tbsp turmeric |

Cut beans into uniform lengths. Cook 1/2 hour in salt water. Drain well. Mix dry ingredients with a little vinegar to form a smooth batter and stir this batter into the boiling vinegar to make smooth paste. Add the beans, boil for 5 minutes and seal.

## SURSILD (PICKLED HERRING)

| | |
|---|---|
| 4 lg salt herring | 1/2 tsp. sugar |
| 1 C. vinegar | 2 lg onions |
| 1 C. water | 6 bay leaves |
| 1 Tbsp whole pepper | |

Wash herring well. Skin and remove bones. Cut into small pieces. Mix vinegar, water and sugar. Add herring, sliced onion, pepper and bay leaves. Let stand over night in a cool place.

*A Norwegian favorite!*

## WATERMELON PICKLES

Peel and cut away pink center from watermelon rind. Cut into chunks about one inch long. Soak in salt water overnight. In the morning, drain. Boil until tender in clear water to which one tablespoon alum has been added. Drain and let come to a boil in clear water. Drain again. Boil in the following prepared juice for fifteen minutes. Seal.

Juice

| | |
|---|---|
| 5 C. vinegar | 2 sticks cinnamon |
| 2 C. water | 1 Tbsp whole cloves |
| 7 C. sugar | 1 Tbsp whole allspice |

*Collect rinds after family reunion picnics.*

# JELLO

Red and yellow, black and white, and green too.

## ODE TO JELLO

Every ethnic group would have a cheer;
The Germans toast, "Hail to our beer!"
Lutefisk and lefse can place the blame
On certain Scandinavians for their fame.

But a little-known food could find a place
In this never-ending battle for first place;
The cry could be heard from the young and old:
"Time to serve JELLO - take it out of the mold."

Give me a "J" and an "E", double "L" and an "O",
Come on your Norskies, your moving too slow.
This is a salad, not a main dish,
Watch so it won't melt into the fish.

Bananas are an added treat
Carefully sliced into the JELLO to eat;
Rise up and be counted as a true ] boy,
JELLO is the dish that reminds you of joy.

It giggles and wiggles and bounces around;
It slips off your fork without making a sound;
You can always remember the last call each day:
"Did you all have your fill of JELLO today?"

When relatives came, there was a new treat:
The JELLO was topped with whipped cream - "Let's eat!"
"Not so fast", - I felt my hand sting - and it hurt!
"it's no longer salad - now it's dessert!"

So let's give a cheer for that American treat
That all Scandinavians soon learn to eat;
"Pass the JELLO," I can still hear it said:
And remember the color - it has to be red!

# RED JELLO

## EVERYDAY JELLO

1 small box Jello
1 C hot water
1 C cold water

Dissolve Jello in hot water. Add cold water and set. This recipe can be doubled.

*A basic Lutheran Jello.*

## JELLO FOR A CROWD

4 boxes Jello
4 C hot water
4 C cold water

Dissolve Jello in hot water. Be careful to get everything dissolved. Add cold water and refrigerate. When partially set, carefully slice in 1 good sized banana or 2 small.

*This will feed about 30 people and is good for funerals or other doings. (This recipe was used for the 75th anniversary of the Trinity Lutheran Church).*

## COMPANY JELLO

1 box red Jello (either strawberry or cherry)
1 C hot water
1 C cold water

Dissolve Jello in hot water. Add cold water and partially set in refrigerator. Slice banana. (Follow directions for "Jello for a Crowd.") Before serving, top with whipped cream!

*This is good for Sunday night supper when company drops in.*

# ROSY VANILLA WHIP

1 pkg raspberry flavored gelatin    1 pkg vanilla pudding
2 C water    2 C milk

Prepare the raspberry-flavored gelatin with two cups water as directed on package. Prepare vanilla pudding with two cups milk as directed on package. Chill gelatin until slightly thickened. Chill pudding. Place the bowl of gelatin in bowl of ice and water and whip with rotary beater until fluffy and the consistency of whipped cream. Add pudding gradually, beating constantly until blended. Turn into sherbert glasses or large serving dish. Chill until firm. Garnish with cubes of clear gelatin or fresh fruit. Serves 10 to 12.

*If you're gutsy, try other flavors of gelatin for variety.*

# CRANBERRY SALAD

1 pkg cherry Jello    2 C water

When dissolved and nearly cold, add 1/2 lb. freshly ground cranberries. When nearly set, add finely cut nuts and marshmallows.

*A Lutheran Thanksgiving Jello.*

# YELLOW JELLO

## CABBAGE AND PINEAPPLE SALAD

1 pkg lemon Jello
1 1/2 C hot water
2 C cabbage, chopped

1 C pineapple, grated
1 C cucumbers, diced

Dissolve lemon Jello in hot water, add to other ingredients, pour into mold. When set, turn out on lettuce to serve. Top with dressing.

*Germans like this one!*


## JELLO DESSERT

3 eggs
1/2 C sugar
1 sm can crushed pineapple

1 pkg lemon Jello
12 graham crackers
1/2 C melted butter

Make crust by adding two tablespoons sugar, butter, to 12 crushed graham crackers. Line pie tin. Add one-third cup sugar and the pineapple to the egg yolks which have been beaten thick. Cook in double boiler until thick and light in color. Pour liquid mixture boiling hot over one package of lemon Jello. Stir and mix well. Add three teaspoons sugar to stiffly beaten egg whites and fold into Jello mixture. Fill lined pie tin with Jello mixture and sprinkle with a crumb topping. Serve with whipped cream. To vary, use peaches, cherries, strawberries or raspberries. Use same flavor in Jello as the fruit. Serves 10.

*Great for Circle!*

## PINEAPPLE SET SALAD

1 pkg lemon Jello
1 C boiling water
1 No. 2 can crushed pineapple
1 C pineapple juice
1 sm glass pimento, cut fine

3/4 C diced celery
1/4 C grated cheese
  (American)
1 C whipping cream
1 Tbsp salad dressing

Dissolve Jello in boiling water and pineapple juice. When this starts to set, add pineapple, pimento, cheese and celery. Add whipped cream to which the salad dressing has been added. Whip all together. Chill. Serve on lettuce with mayonnaise dressing. Serves 12.

*A wedding shower treat!*


## SALAD EXCELLENT

1 pkg lemon Jello
Juice from 1 lg can crushed
  pineapple
2 pkgs. Philadelphia Cream
  Cheese

1 sm can pimento
1/2 C chopped celery
1/8 tsp salt
1/2 pint whipping cream
2/3 C walnuts, chopped

Boil pineapple juice and add to the Jello. Let cool until slightly thick. Add the crushed pineapple. Cream cheese with pimento, add celery and walnuts, and add to the Jello. Fold in the cream beaten stiff and place in refrigerator till firm. Serves 10.

# BLACK JELLO

## BLACK CHERRY JELLO DESSERT

1/2 lb vanilla wafers
1 lb marshmallows
1 No. 2 can pie cherries
   (pitted)

1 C milk
1 pkg black cherry Jello
1 pkg strawberry Jello
1 pint whipping cream

Crush wafers fine. Cook marshmallows and milk until marshmallows melt. Let cool. Heat cherries to boiling point. Drain. Add enough water to cherry juice to make 4 cups liquid. Dissolve the two packages of Jello in this liquid. When Jello starts to set, add cherries. Fold in 1/2 of whipped cream (1 cup) into cooled marshmallow mixture. To mold, spread half of crushed wafers in bottom of pan. Cover with marshmallow filling. Add Jello with cherries. to form second layer. For third layer, whip the remaining cream, sweeten slightly and put on top of cherry layer. Sprinkle the top with remaining crushed wafers. Chill in refrigerator until firm. If you want to slice your dessert, mold in a nut bread tin. Serves 16.

*A dark colored Jello nice to serve when other races are present. It makes them feel welcome in Lutheran circles.*

# *WHITE JELLO*

## YUM YUM SALAD

2 Tbsp gelatin
1/2 C water
1 C crushed pineapple
1/2 C sugar
1 Tbsp lemon juice

1 C grated cheese
1 C whipped cream
2 Tbsp chopped green
    peppers

Soak gelatin in 1/2 cup water for ten minutes. Heat the crushed pineapple and mix well with the gelatin. Add the sugar and lemon juice. Chill until partially set and fold in the cheese, peppers and whipped cream. Pour in molds and chill until set. Serve garnished with lettuce and mayonnaise. Serves 8.

*This goes good with lutefisk, lefse, and mashed potatoes if you prefer to keep all your food white. Some Norwegian Lutherans like it this way.*

## AND GREEN TOO

### CHRISTMAS PACKAGE SALAD

1 pkg lime Jello
1 1/2 C hot water
1/2 C chopped celery
1 C peas

1 C cabbage, finely
　shredded
1/2 C carrots, grated
lettuce

Dissolve Jello in hot water, let set slightly, add vegetables. Pour into loaf pan, let set, cut in squares and serve on lettuce. Place strips of pimento across the serving of salad as if tied with red ribbon. If a red salad base is used, decorate with strips of green pepper.

*A clever Lutheran figured this one out.*

### GREEN SALAD

1 pkg lime Jello
2 Tbsp chopped carrots
1 C cream, whipped
1 C cottage cheese

1 C Miracle Whip
onion and olives, chopped
　as desired

Mix lime Jello according to directions, let set slightly, then whip. Add remaining ingredients, pour into molds and chill.

*Can be served with or without mayonnaise, depending upon how fancy the people are the you are serving.*

### JELLO SALAD

1 pkg lime Jello
1 pkg lemon Jello
1/2 tsp salt
1 Tbsp lemon juice
1 med can pineapple
1 sm celery stalk

1 med can white cherries
1 sm bottle stuffed olives
　(sliced)
2 carrots, chopped fine
1 sm cabbage, chopped fine

Dissolve Jello in three cups of hot water. Add all other ingredients and chill. Serves 12.

*The white cherries make this a little "spendy".*

## LIME SALAD

1 pkg lime Jello
1 1/2 C boiling water
3/4 C whipping cream
1 C cottage cheese
1 med sized cucumber

1 tsp vinegar or lemon
   juice
1/2 green pepper
3 med sized carrots
1/2 C salad dressing
   (Miracle Whip)

Dissolve Jello in boiling water. Cool until partially set. Grind vegetables and add to Jello mixture. Whip cottage cheese until smooth and combine with whipped cream. Add to Jello mixture and chill until set. Cut in squares and serve on lettuce with or without salad dressing. Serves 8.

*You be the judge.*

## UNDER-THE-SEA PEAR SALAD

1 pkg lime Jello
1 1/2 C boiling water
1/2 C pear juice
1/4 tsp salt
1/8 tsp ginger

1 tsp vinegar or lemon
   juice
2 C diced pears
1 pkg Philadelphia cream
   cheese

Dissolve Jello in boiling water. Add pear juice, salt and vinegar. Pour half in mold and chill. Let other stand until jelly-like. Beat in cheese and ginger, and fold in pears. Add on top of other layer.

*Some Lutherans call this Pharoah's Army Jello.*

42

## JELLO AND VEGETABLES

1 box Jello
1 C hot water
1 C cold water

Dissolve Jello in hot water. Add cold water and pour into aluminum mold. Refrigerate. When partially set, carefully add 2 small or 1 large grated carrot, 1 stalk chopped celery. Set till firm. Before serving, carefully remove from mold and serve with salad dressing.

*This is good for showers.*

## JELLO RECIPES AND TIPS
## THAT DIDN'T FIT IN THE OTHER
## CATEGORIES

### JELLO FOR SILVER WEDDINGS AND
### OTHER SPECIAL HOLIDAY DOINGS

3 boxes Jello
3 C hot water
3 C cold water

Dissolve Jello in hot water. Add cold water and pour into aluminum mold and refrigerate. When partially set, carefully add drained fruit cocktail, banana, marshmallows or any other favorite ingredients for Jello. Before serving, carefully remove from mold and add whipped cream. Serve.

### JELLO STRETCHING

1 box Jello
1 C hot water
1 1/2 C cold water

Dissolve Jello in hot water. Add cold water and set. This recipe can be used if you need a little bit more Jello.


*Lutherans serve green Jello with fish.*

44

# SALADS

Pineapple and rice

Refreshing and nice

# SALADS

## COLESLAW

8 C cabbage, finely shredded
   with knife
2 carrots, shredded

1 green pepper, chopped
1/2 C finely chopped
   onion

Sprinkle vegetables with 1/2 cup cold water and place in refrigerator for at least 1/2 hour. Dissolve 1 envelope Knox Gelatin in 1/4 cup cold water.

2/3 C sugar
2/3 C vinegar
1 tsp celery salt

1 tsp salt
1/4 tsp black pepper
2/3 C oil

Mix sugar, vinegar and spices and bring to a boil. Stir in softened gelatin. Cool until slightly thickened. Beat well. Gradually beat in oil. Pour over chilled vegetables. This makes a large bowl full and keeps for days. Stir before each use.

## GLORIFIED RICE

1 box of lemon gelatin
1 C boiling water
1 C or less of crushed
   pineapple

2 C boiled rice (dry)
1 C cream
4 or 5 Tbsp sugar
salt to taste

Dissolve gelatine in boiling water, when cool and thickened whip to consistency of heavy cream. Add the rice, pineapple and whipped cream sugar and salt. Pour into any desired mold to set. When cool and set, unmold on serving plate. Garnish with whipped cream and red or green cherries. Makes about ten servings.

## PINEAPPLE AND RICE

2 C cooked rice                          1 C raw apples (chopped)
1 C crushed pineapple (drained)          1/2 C sugar
24 marshmallows (cut up)                 1 C heavy cream

Cook rice in boiling salted water. Drain. Cool and mix with
pineapple, marshmallows, apple, and sugar. Place in refrigerator
until serving time. Then fold in cream which has been whipped.
Garnish with candied cherries, sliced bananas, or other fruit.

## MANDARIN ORANGE SALAD

2 pkg (3 oz.) orange jello               1 1/2 C hot water
1 C boiling water                        1 can mandarin oranges
2 C vanilla ice cream                      and juice

Dissolve one package of orange Jello and one cup boiling water.
Add two cups vanilla ice cream. Stir well. Pour into 9 inch
square pan and chill.

Dissolve one package of orange Jello in 1 1/2 cups hot water.
Add mandarin oranges and juice. Chill until syrupy. Pour over
first layer. Chill. cut into serving squares.

## MUSTARD RING SALAD

4 eggs beaten
2 Tbsp mustard
1 C whipping cream (whipped)
3/4 C vinegar (fill with water
   to equal 1 cup)
1 to 1 1/2 C shredded cabbage

3/4 C sugar
1 envelope gelatin
1/2 C water (to dissolve
   gelatin)
pinch of salt

Mix dry ingredients, add vinegar/water mixture; mix well and add beaten eggs. Dissolve gelatine in water in double boiler and stir until melted; add eggs mixture and cook until creamy, stirring constantly. Cool. Fold in whipped cream and cabbage. Pour into greased mold or tube pan and refrigerate.

*Simply delicious with ham!!*

HISTORY: The Sodality ladies ham dinner was memorable, not for its ham and good scalloped potatoes, but for its delicious Mustard Ring Salad.

## POTATO SALAD FOR 100

Boil up 32 pounds of potatoes. Chill. Add 4 bunches of celery, 4 dozen hard boiled eggs, 8 green peppers, pickles, salad dressing and salt and pepper to taste. Recipe can be doubled for big crowds.

*A Sunday School Picnic MUST!!*

# HOTDISHES

# HOTDISHES

## HOT DISH FOR SOCIALS OR AID

1 medium chicken
1 cup diced celery
6 or 8 hard cooked eggs diced
1 tsp salt
1/8 tsp pepper

1 quart chicken broth
1 C. cream
4 Tbsp. flour
1 Tbsp. water

Cook chicken, remove bones and cut meat in small pieces. Butter baking dish and put in layers of chicken, celery and eggs until all are used. Add the cream to the chicken broth, bring to a boil and thicken with the flour, mixed with the water, until smooth. Pour sauce over chicken mixture and top with cracker or bread crumbs. Bake until browned on top. Bake at 300 degrees for 1 hour. This serves 15 and is as timeless as you can get. Mrs. P.W. ( Peder Walter) Sorenson always skimped and used milk instead of real cream.

*Everyone could tell but never said anything. It wasn't the only thing she skimped on.*

## CHICKEN

## CAN ADD CHICKEN RICE HOT DISH

2 C. cooked rice
1/2 C. chopped parsley
4 small onions
1 tsp. salt

2 C. grated cheese
2 eggs, beaten
3 C. milk

Mix rice, parsley, onions, cheese and salt; then mix eggs, milk and add to the rest. Bake in buttered dish. Bake at 350 degrees for 1 hour. Serves 6-8.

*To make this without chicken would be foolish, would be nothing in the recipe that would stick to the ribs. This is especially important to remember when serving funerals where there are men eating.*

## CHICKEN HOT DISH

1 chicken
1 pkg ring macaroni

2 C. milk
2 Tbsp butter

1 can peas
1 can mushroom soup

3 hard boiled eggs

Boil chicken until well done; remove meat from bones and dice. Cook macaroni rings. Grease casserole and put macaroni, peas, diced chicken and mushroom soup in layers. Make a white sauce of the butter, flour and milk and pour over. Top with bread crumbs or shredded wheat. Bake for 40 minutes.

*The shredded wheat gives this recipe some much needed bulk. If you bake too long the peas become mushy.*

## CHICKEN, VEAL OR TURKEY ROYAL
### Fit for King Olaf

1 C. chopped mushrooms
4 Tbsp butter
1 Tbsp flour
1/2 C. bread crumbs
1 1/4 C. chopped cooked chicken,
    turkey, or veal

3/4 C. milk
2 Tbsp chopped parsley
3 eggs
1/2 tsp. salt
pepper

Dredge mushrooms with flour and brown in tow tablespoons butter. Scald milk, add remaining butter and crumbs. Cool, add remaining ingredients and pour into buttered shallow pan, set in pan of hot water and bake until firm. Cut in squares. Serve with cheese sauce.

Cheese Sauce
2 Tbsp butter
2 Tbsp flour

1 C. milk
1/2 C. grated cheese

Melt butter, add flour and blend. Add milk and cook over low heat, stirring constantly. Remove from flame and stir in cheese. Bake at 350 degrees for 45 minutes.

*This isn't an everyday hot dish and is too time consuming to make for and ordinary church function. If the church higher-ups are visiting, this would be appropriate.*

## CHICKEN HOT DISH

| | |
|---|---|
| 2 C. cooked chicken | chicken broth |
| 1 C. cream | 1/2 can peas |
| | |
| 3 C. cracker crumbs | pepper and salt to taste, little grated onion if desired. |

Alternate layers of chicken, peas and crumbs until dish is filled. Pour cream and broth over to cover the layers. Top with crumbs. Bake in moderate over about 40 minutes.

*This is a basic chicken hot dish. Any kind of crumbs on the top will do.*

## CHICKEN LOAF

| | |
|---|---|
| 1 C. cooked spaghetti | 1/4 C. grated cheese |
| 1 C. cooked diced chicken | 1/4 C. chopped green |
| 1 C. bread crumbs | peppers |
| 1 1/2 C. warm milk | 2 Tbsp chopped pimento |
| 1/4 C. melted butter | 1 tsp. salt |
| 1 can mushroom soup | 3 eggs, beaten slightly |
| 1/2 cup of milk | |

Saute green pepper in butter. Mix all ingredients except mushroom soup. Bake in loaf pan. Slice and top with hot cream of mushroom soup diluted with milk. Bake for 60 minutes.

*This is pretty fancy and would be good for a shower - wedding or baby.*

## ESCALLOPED CHICKEN

| | |
|---|---|
| 4 C. cubed chicken | 1/1/4 tsp. sage |
| 4 C. broth | 1/4 C. cream or chicken |
| 4 Tbsp flour | stock |

55

| | |
|---|---|
| 4 Tbsp chicken fat | 3/4 tsp. salt |
| 6 C. bread crumbs | 1/2 tsp. pepper |
| 3/4 C. melted butter | 2 Tbsp. chopped onion |

Cook chicken in salted water, cool and cut into 1 inch cubes. Make a dressing of bread cut into 1 inch squares, melted butter, or chicken fat, sage, stock or cream, salt, pepper and onion. Make gravy of broth from which fat has been removed, flour and chicken fat. Put 1 1/2 inch layers of chicken in oiled pan. Cover with dry dressing. Pour gravy over top and bake at 375 degrees for 35 minutes.

*This is a "meat and potato" chicken recipe and is good for pot lucks.*

## GRANDMA CARLSON'S CHICKEN HOT DISH

| | |
|---|---|
| 1 large chicken | 1 can peas |
| 1 C. dice carrots | 1 small onion |
| 1 C. diced potatoes | 1 C. diced celery |
| salt and pepper to taste | |

Cook chicken until done. Bone and dice chicken; use broth to make gravy. Put all in layers in a casserole with a sprinkle of flour between layers. Add broth last and a little cream and bake.

*This one could use this new bought Cream of Chicken soup. This is an old recipe so it could be changed.*

## CORN HOT DISH

| | |
|---|---|
| 1 lb. ground beef | 2 Tbsp butter |
| 1 small onion, chopped | 1/2 tsp. salt |
| 1 can whole kernel corn | 1/8 tsp. pepper |
| 1 small green pepper, chopped | 2 Tbsp flour |
| 1 can tomato soup | 3 Tbsp water |

Brown the meat and onion in the butter. Add rest of ingredients and simmer on top of the stove for twenty minutes. Use the flour mixed with the water for thickening.

*If you have corn from your garden, all the better.*

## DAGNE'S DINNER IN A DISH

4 Tbsp. shortening
1 medium onion sliced
2 green peppers, diced
1 lb. hamburger
2 C. fresh cut corn

1 1/2 tsp salt
1/4 tsp pepper
2 eggs
1/2 C. dry bread crumbs
3. or 4 tomatoes

Fry onions and peppers slightly. Blend in meat and seasoning. Remove from fire. Stir in eggs and mix well. Put a cup of corn in a buttered baking dish, cover with one half of the meat and a layer of tomatoes. Repeat. Bake for 35 minutes at 350 degrees.

*If you don't have green peppers, skip it. Some men don't like them.*

## GLORIFIED HAMBURGER

2 C. or 1 lb hamburger (all beef)
1/2 tsp. baking powder
sprinkle of pepper
milk to moisten

1 C. bread crumbs
1/2 tsp. salt
2 Tbsp catsup

Mix crumbs, seasonings, baking powder and catsup with meat. Add enough milk to moisten sufficiently to mold into cakes. Put a strip of thin bacon around each and fasten with a toothpick. Put butter on top. Bake in hot oven 45 minutes

*This is heavenly and fit for the angels. This isn't something that Lutheran Church Basement Women make for church doings, but Lutheran Church Basement Women do make it.*

## HAMBURGER PIE

1 lb. hamburger
1 can tomato soup
1 can peas

1 can whole kernel corn
1 large onion

Fry hamburger and onions stirring until brown. Put into rectangular pan with corn, peas and soup. Season highly with salt and pepper. Boil about one dozen potatoes and mash until fluffy. Add 1 beaten egg. Put a scoop of this over top of meat mixture for individual servings. Sprinkle with paprika. Bake in a hot oven about 20 minutes.

*Even though it might resemble apple crisp a la mode, it isn't. A clever way to serve meat and potatoes even though you can't technically call it a "hot dish." Mrs. Olaf Hanson though this up when she was in the hospital recovering from pleurisy and other complications.*

## HAMBURGER-RICE HOT DISH

Brown one pound hamburger and 3/4 cup of raw rice in 2 or 3 Tbsp. fat. Put in casserole with one cup of chopped onion, one cup of finely minced celery, four cups of tomato juice. Season with pepper and one tsp. each of curry powder and salt. Mix together thoroughly and bake, covered in a moderate oven for one and one half hours at 350 degrees. Stir occasionally.

*Some Lutheran Women don't like or stock curry powder, so if you don't, it doesn't make any difference.*

## HELGA'S HOT DISH

| | |
|---|---|
| 6 potatoes, sliced | 1 lb. hamburger |
| 1 can tomatoes | 4 onions, sliced |
| 1 can cream style corn | salt and pepper |

Arrange potatoes and onions in baking pan. Season. Fry meat, add tomatoes and corn. Pour over potatoes and onions. Bake until potatoes are tender.

*Sometimes when Helga brought this to Aid Meetings she didn't bake it long enough and the potatoes were hard. Once persnickety Miss Esther Mae Skogen tried to cut the potato at Ladies Aid and it flew off her plate and landed in the late Mr.s A.K. Olson's lap. Everyone saw it and thought it's about time; she was always acting so perfect and criticizing everyone's kids.*

## HOT HAMBURGER DISH

| | |
|---|---|
| 1 1/2 lbs hamburger | 2 C. raw diced potatoes |
| 2 Tbsp. fat | 1 C. diced celery |
| 1 onion | 1 can tomato soup |
| 2 C. fresh peas | 1/2 tsp. salt |
| 2 C. raw diced carrots | 1/8 tsp. pepper |

Brown the meat and diced onion in the fat. Add tomato soup, vegetables, salt and pepper. Bake in buttered baking dish. Bake at 350 degrees for 45 minutes.

*It serves 10 and is called hot hamburger dish supreme instead of just the hamburger dish, because it calls for 1/2 pound more hamburger than the normal recipe.*

## LEFT OVER MEAT DISH

Make a regular bread dressing using about four of five cups bread crumbs. Grind up any left over meats such as beef, veal or pork. Place about half of the meat in bottom of a buttered baking dish. Cover with the dressing and the remainder of the meat and bake till slightly browned on top. Bake at 350 degrees for 35 minutes.

*A good way to use up old bread and left over meat and still have a tasty dish. Waste not. Want not.*

## MEAT AND VEGETABLE HOT DISH

| | |
|---|---|
| 1 1/2 lb. round steak | 1 C. creamed style corn |
| 1/2 C. grated cheese | 1/2 lb. pork |
| 1 C. tomato soup | 2 eggs |
| 1/2 C. onions | 1 C. mushroom soup |
| 1/2 green pepper | |

Grind pork and steak together. Mix with other ingredients and heat thoroughly. Serve on 1 1/2 lbs. chow mein noodles.

*It doesn't sound good to mix cream style corn, tomato soup and cream of mushroom soup, but you can trust a tried and true Lutheran Church Basement Women's recipe.*

## NOODLE AND HAMBURGER HOT DISH
### For Funerals

| | |
|---|---|
| 1 lb hamburger | 1 onion |
| 1 pkg. egg noodles | 1 can vegetable soup |
| 1 tsp. salt | 1 can tomato soup |
| 1/8 tsp. pepper | |

Fry hamburger and onions until brown. Add seasoning. Cook and drain the noodles. Mix together the meat, noodles and soups. Add 1 cup of water. Bake in buttered casserole. Any left over cooked vegetables may be added to this dish. Bake at 350 degrees for 1 hour.

*If you don't have egg noodles use elbow macaroni for any other sensible macaroni you have on hand.*

## NOODLE HOT DISH
### For Funerals

| | |
|---|---|
| 5 slices bacon | 1 C. peas and juice |
| 1 1/4 lbs. hamburger | 1/2 C. mushrooms |
| 1 small onion diced | 1 pkg. egg noodles |
| 1 C. tomato soup | 1/2 tsp. salt |

Fry bacon and remove from pan. Fry hamburger and onions. Add tomato soup, peas, mushrooms and salt. Mix all together and add noodles which have been cooked. Pour into buttered casserole. Place bacon strips over top. Bake at 400 degrees for 20 minutes.

*Remember don't drain the peas! You need the pea juice for this one.*

## SIX LAYER HOT DISH

| | |
|---|---|
| 2 C. raw potatoes | 1 lb. hamburger |
| 2 C. diced celery | 2 C. tomato |
| 1 C. diced onion | 1/2 tsp. salt |
| 1/2 C. diced green pepper (optional) | 1/8 tsp. pepper (or less) |

Arrange into layers with seasoned uncooked hamburger made into balls on top of dish. Bake at 350 degrees for 1 1/2 hours.

*If you skip the green peppers, which are optional, you only have a 5 layer hot dish; but Lutheran Church Basement Women still call it Six Layer Hot Dish.*

## SUNDAY SCHOOL CASSEROLE

| | |
|---|---|
| 1 6-oz pkg. macaroni or spaghetti | 1 1/2 C. milk |
| | 3 Tbsp. butter |
| 1/4 lb. dried beef | 1 C. grated American cheese |
| 3 Tbsp. flour | 1 green pepper |

Cook macaroni according to directions. Drain. Frizzle meat and cook green pepper in butter. Add flour and blend. Add milk and cook until thick stirring constantly. Add 3/4 of cheese. Combine sauce and macaroni. Top with remaining cheese. Bake 30 to 40 minutes at 350 degrees.

*Only a Lutheran Church Basement Woman would know how to frizzle dried beef and frizzle it right. Sunday School kids like lots of cheese and no green peppers if you're making it for them.*

## TEXAS HASH

| | |
|---|---|
| 2 C. sliced onion | 1 lb. ground beef |
| 1 No. 2 can tomatoes | 1 tsp. salt |
| 3 Tbsp. fat | 1/2 C. uncooked rice |
| 3/4 C. chopped green pepper | 1/2 tsp. chili powder |

Cook onion and green pepper in fat until onion is soft and yellow. Add meat and brown. Add remaining ingredients. Pour in greased casserole. Bake 1 hour at 350 degrees.

*If you are a Lutheran from Texas this might work out, but if you're a Lutheran from the Midwest, the chili powder isn't going to win you any awards at most Midwest Lutheran functions.*

| | |
|---|---|
| 2 lg. onions, sliced fine | 1/2 C. uncooked rice |
| 2 green peppers, cut fine | 1 tsp. chili powder |
| 3 Tbsp. butter or Spry | 1 tsp. salt |
| 1 lb. ground beef | 1/4 tsp. pepper |
| 2 C. canned tomatoes | |

Brown meat, onions and peppers in the butter and mix well. Add the tomatoes, rice, chili powder, salt and pepper. Bake in buttered casserole. Bake at 375 degrees for 45 minutes.

*Tillie Thorstad moved from Decorah to Texas and started cooking different. She sent this recipe thinking we didn't have it in the Midwest. Evelyn Peterson thanked her for the recipe, but also told her we already had the recipe and some had been making it for several years. She also added Midwest Lutheran Women didn't' make it on a regular basis because people here work hard and can't afford to stay up all night with heartburn from chili powder.*

# PORK

## HOTDISH DELUXE

| | |
|---|---|
| 1 lb lean pork | 1 small glass pimento |
| 1 can chicken soup | 1 can cream style corn |
| 1 cup water | 1/2 lb cream cheese |
| 2 small packages noodles | 1 cup bread crumbs |

Bake at 325 degrees for 45 minutes.

*Mr. and Mrs Ole Ingebritson and their neighbors, Mr. and Mrs. Jens Olson went together and gave the pastor a half a hog for Christmas. The pastor's wife experimented around with all the pork she had and came up with this recipe she served when visiting pastors were guests in her home. Once when she brought it for Aid, everyone hinted for the recipe by telling her how delicious it was; but no one had the nerve to ask her except for Mrs. Andrew Olafson who dares to ask anything. The pastor's wife was gracious enough to give it to her.*


# TUNA

## POTATO CHIPS AND TUNA HOT DISH

| | |
|---|---|
| 1/2 pound potato chips | 1 can mushroom soup |
| 1 7-oz can tuna fish | 1 C. hot milk |
| 1 small can peas | |

Put alternate layers of potato chips, tuna, and peas in a buttered baking dish. Add milk to the soup and pour over ingredients in casserole. Bake at 350 degrees for 1 hour.

*This is good for Dorcas society lunch or any other light supper meal served in church.*

## SNAPPY TUNA RING

| | |
|---|---|
| 2 C. noodles cooked | 4 eggs |
| 1/4 lb. snappy cheese | 1 1/2 C. milk |

1 can tuna fish                          1 tsp. salt

Fill 1 1/2-quart ring mold in layers with noodles, snappy cheese and tuna fish. Add beaten eggs, mixed with milk and salt. Place mold in pan of hot water and bake. Unmold. Fill center of ring with buttered or creamed peas. Melt cheese to smooth sauce in double boiler. Pour cheese over top and serve at once. Bake at 350 degrees for 1 hour.

*The cheese is what makes this snappy. You'll need a lot of workers to serve this one so everyone can eat it hot. Everyone at Aid will ooh and aah over this one, that's for sure.*

## TUNA FISH HOT DISH

1 10 cent pkg. potato chips          1 can tuna fish
1 can mushroom soup                  2 hard cooked eggs

Drain all oil from tuna fish, flake, and mix with the mushroom soup and crushed potato chips. Put in greased casserole. Place slices of hard cooked eggs over top. Bake at 325 degrees for 45 minutes.

*Potato chips have gone up in price since this was written, but what hasn't.*

# VEAL

## SPECIAL HOT DISH

1 lb. ground veal                    1 1/2 C. diced celery
1/2 C. rice                          1 small can mushrooms
1 can cream of mushroom soup         3 Tbsp butter
1 can chicken rice soup              1/2 tsp. salt
1 C. water                           1/8 tsp. pepper
1 onion, diced

Brown the onion, celery and meat in the butter; add the rice (uncooked), mushrooms, soups and water. Season with salt and pepper. Bake. The last half hour sprinkle with 1/2 cup chopped salted almonds, if desired. Bake at 325 degrees for 1 1/2 hours.

*Mrs. Hans Olson said her sister-in-law's neighbor in Seattle had the church women serve this at her daughters wedding. (The sister-in-law of Mrs. Hans Olson sent the recipe to Mrs. Hans Olson) She said the woman always lived beyond her means and always tried to impress everyone even though she was born and raised in a conservative Lutheran family. Lutheran Church Basement Women don't serve this in church, but some said they like to read how the other half of the world lives and cooks.*

## INTERNATIONAL

### CHOP SUEY

| | |
|---|---|
| 18 stalks celery | 6 C. water or meat stock |
| 1 lb. fresh tomatoes | 5 lbs. bermuda onions |
| 2 1/2 C. cornstarch | 2 green peppers |
| 5 lbs. pork, cut for chop suey | 3/4 C. molasses |
| 1/4 oz. can pimentos | 3 lbs. veal cut for chop |
| 3 1/2 C. Chinese sauce | suey |
| 6 lbs. rice | 6 No. 2 cans bean sprouts |

Cook diced celery and sliced onions with water or meat stock until vegetables are soft but not completely cooked. Brown meat in two Tbsp. fat. While meat is browning drain liquid from celery and onions and mix the Chinese sauce, molasses and cornstarch. Cook on high until it boils then add the meat and let sauce continue to cook until starchy taste is gone or about 30 minutes. Add the bean sprouts which have been drained, celery and onions and cook until thoroughly heated; then add tomatoes, green peppers and pimentos which have been cut in thin strips. Serve on boiled rice or Chinese fried noodles (Serves 50 with portion of 3/4 cup each).

*This isn't a favorite with Lutheran men but the world is getting smaller all the time and we can't live in our own little world.*

## CHOW MEIN

3 lbs. round steak
1 lb. veal
1 lb. pork
1 No. 2 can subgum
1 8-oz can mushrooms
1 Tbsp. molasses
1/4 C. lard or drippings

2 medium bunches celery
2 large onions
1 No. 2 can bean sprouts
3 cans noodles
3 Tbsp. soy sauce
1 tsp. salt
1 tsp. pepper

Dice meat, brown well in drippings; cook slowly, with one cup water added, for one hour. Add celery and onions cut in small pieces, salt, and pepper. Thicken with two tablespoons flour mixed with three tablespoons water. Serve on hot crisp noodles. (For Chicken Chow Mein, use 3 pounds diced chicken, 1 pound veal and 1 pound pork.)

*Some grocery stores don't carry subgum or bean sprouts, but you can get by without them. Chow Mein isn't served in the Lutheran Church, but it is gaining in popularity as an okay dish from the Orient. Someday in the future it might be as popular as hot dishes.*

## MEXICAN GOULASH

1 lb. bacon
1 can corn
1 can lima beans

1 box spaghetti or noodles
1 can tomatoes
1 can peas

Prepare spaghetti or noodles according to directions on box. Fry the bacon and add it to the drippings. Then add corn, tomatoes, lima beans and peas. (Drain the liquid from the beans and peas). Season to taste.

*Lutheran Women use this recipe in a pinch.*

## SPANISH RICE

1/4 lb. bacon
3 C. boiled rice
1/2 tsp. celery salt

1-3 C. chopped onions
1/2 tsp. salt
2 1/2 C. tomatoes

66

Cut bacon into small pieces. Brown in frying pan. Add onions and brown with bacon. Add rest of ingredients and pour in casserole and bake for about 45 minutes.

*Most Lutherans prefer their rice "glorified". Some aren't comfortable with Spanish rice, but some are.*

# LUTHERAN BARS

# WHY LUTHERANS CALL THEIR DESSERTS - BARS

Most Lutheran women have heard this story for years. As time went on, some fabrications and half-truths crept into this tale, but if you can overlook some minor exaggerations here and there, this story makes sense.

Once upon a time Martin Luther's mother said to him, "Why don't you take Kitty and the kids up to Norway to visit my third cousin, Ingebrit Martinson and her son Lars? She wrote me last Christmas and said she didn't know how much time she had left, and she'd like you and your family to see their new Lutheran church."

So Martin and Kitty packed up Martin Jr., baby sister Olga, and some sandwiches and set off for Norway. Third cousin Ingebrit was so excited they were coming she told all her neighbors and they decided to honor Martin and his family with a pot-luck supper in the basement of their new Lutheran church - First Lutheran of Stavanger.

Meanwhile, Martin Luther's mother was glad to see Martin and his family go to Norway so she could have a little peace and quiet. Martin had created such a fuss in Germany, she couldn't sleep. Even though she knew in her heart Martin was "in the right", she was sure others were talking about him, and this caused her blood pressure to rise. (Martin's mother had a small amount of Norwegian blood in her veins which caused her to feel uneasy when anyone in her family was thrust in the limelight.)

When Martin and his family arrived at Ingebrit's home, everyone was happy and excited except Ingebrit's son, Lars. Famous people made him feel nervous and uneasy, and he didn't know how he should act. So he just acted the same, got up, and went outside to do the chores.

Ingebrit put on the egg coffee, brought out dried beef sandwiches, cheese, herring, buns, pickles, and desserts for a little snack. After Ingebrit apologized for not having "ing a ting" on hand to serve, they all started to visit. Kitty was nervous because the kids were tired, crabby, and restless after the long journey. She was hoping they wouldn't act up too bad. Martin Luther's mother had warned Kitty to watch Martin too. He was always whistling "A Mighty Fortress", and in Norway, whistling was the same as calling the devil.

When Lars finished the chores, they all got ready and went to First Lutheran of Stavanger. Kitty was busy spit cleaning her children's faces with her hanky all the way to church. When they arrived, the church was full of men visiting, women cooking, and children running and swinging around the church basement poles. The women in the kitchen, standing on their tip-toes, took turns looking through the little windows in the kitchen doors to try get a glimpse of Martin and his family. Anna Axelson said she thought he wasn't as tall as she had imagined, but that didn't make him less of a Lutheran she supposed. "Oh my," said Tina Severson. "There he stands." Lena Larson said she didn't think Germans were usually as dark skinned as Martin and his family, but she added she'd never remembered seeing a real live German either.

Gurine Olson, President of the Ladies Aid, told the women to go their assigned stations while she told the pastor "vaer sa god." The pastor nodded to her, asked everyone to stand for the blessing and table grace. Everything went fine until they started to sing the last line of the table grace. Gurine Olson had invited all the neighboring Lutheran churches to the pot luck, but because she was so busy getting everything ready, she forgot to ask the pastor to announce what ending to the table grace they would be singing. (Lutheran churches sing different endings).

When some started to sing "May Feast in Paradise with Thee" while simultaneously others were singing "May Strengthen for Thy Service be", Gurine turned beet red and got all embarrassed. She couldn't' dwell on the embarrassment though, because she was in charge of getting everyone through the serving line, she knew Martin didn't know much Norwegian, nobody would explain it to him, and she would just have to think about it later when she went to sleep that night.

Everything went as smooth as could be expected until the desserts were passed around the table for a second time. By this time the kids had gone outside to play, and only the grown-ups were left visiting and drinking coffee. After passing a plate of cake and desserts to the people sitting at Martin's table, Lena Larson scurried back to the kitchen and told everyone that Martin had said to her, "Those Prayer Bars are really good and hit the spot." Lena got all flustered, said tak, and told the women in the kitchen she didn't know how to tell Martin Luther that a bar was not a dessert but a place where outlaws and ruffians would sit and drink hard liquor. Anna Axelson tried to calm down all the servers by telling them that maybe the word bar was the German word for dessert. Tina Severson said maybe Martin was just clearing stuff from his throat and Lean had just imagined Martin said the word bars.

While the women were discussing the issues Kitty Luther walked into the kitchen and asked where the bathroom was located. She had Martin Luther, Jr. standing by her side - his clothes were all dirty and his nose was all bloody. Just then Lena Larson's son came running into the kitchen and said the kids were playing tombstone tag. Martin Jr. had tried to jump over Hans Hauge's large tombstone but he didn't make it. He fell on his face and that's why, according to Lena Larson's son, he got hurt. Lena grabbed her son by the arm, sat him firmly on a chair, gave him that "wait until your father hears about this look, and whispered in his ear to sit still if he knew what was good for himself.

After a few minutes, Kitty Luther came back into the kitchen, thanked the women for letting her use the bathroom, and then to everyone's horror, asked Lena if she would be willing to part with her Prayer Bar recipe. Lena was flattered to be asked for the recipe, but couldn't muster up the courage to tell Kitty that Norwegians and Swedish Lutheran women didn't call their desserts - bars. She was so shaken she didn't have any choice but to write down the recipe - "From the Kitchen of Lena Larson, Prayer Bars."

The rest is history. Since nobody dared to offend Martin Luther or his wife, Lutheran women had no other choice but to call their desserts - bars.

# LUTHERAN BARS

## APPLE BARS

Crust
2 1/2 C. flour
1 tsp. salt
2 Tbsp. sugar

1/2 C butter
1/2 C shortening
2 egg yolks
milk

Mix like pie crust. Put egg yolks into measuring cup and add enough milk to make 2/3 cup and add to first mixture. Roll out half to fit a jelly roll pan (about 10 x 15 inch).

Filling
2/3 C crushed corn flakes
6 to 10 apples

1 1/2 C sugar
1 tsp. cinnamon

Sprinkle the corn flakes over the bottom crust. Slice apples and distribute over crust. Mix sugar and cinnamon and sprinkle over apples. Add the top crust and seal edges by pinching together.

Topping
Beat the two egg whites stiff and spread on crust. Bake 40 minutes in a 350 degrees oven. Make a glaze of 1 cup powdered sugar and a little milk, flavored with vanilla. Dribble over top while hot or melt light Kraft Caramels with 1/2 cup evaporated milk and use this instead of glaze. This may be used as a dessert or bar.

*Aanna Olson said teenagers will clean up a pan of these bars quicker than lightening.*

## CHOCOLATE CHIP BARS

1 C crunchy peanut butter
1/2 C butter

1 C or pkg chocolate chips

Melt together and pour over 1 bag miniature marshmallows. Put in loaf pan and refrigerate. Will keep for a week, but then won't last a week. (Cool the chocolate mixture so it does not melt the marshmallows).

## BRAN DATE BARS

1 C flour (sifted)
1/3 tsp salt
2 tsp Watkins Baking Powder
1 1/2 C sugar
1 C bran
1 1/2 C chopped dates

1 C chopped walnut meats
4 eggs, yolks and whites
    beaten separately
1/4 C milk
1 tsp Watkins Vanilla or
    Almond Extract

Beat egg yolks, beat in sugar. Add sifted dry mixture alternately with milk. Add dates, nuts and lastly, beaten egg whites. Turn into shallow greased baking pan and bake in moderate oven. When cool cut in strips and brush with powdered sugar.

*A treat that helps you become "regular".*

## BROWNIES

1 C butter
2 C brown sugar
4 eggs
8 Tbsp cocoa
1/2 C hot water

1 1/2 C flour
1 tsp baking powder
1/8 tsp salt
1 C nuts (or less)
1 tsp vanilla

Cream shortening, add sugar and cream well. Make a paste of cocoa and hot water. Add eggs, salt, vanilla and cocoa paste; beat well. Sift baking powder with the flour and add chopped nuts. Add to creamed mixture. Spread on buttered cookie sheet, size 14 x 17 inches. Bake. Before brownies are completely cooled, cut into desired size. Bake at 350 degrees for 30 minutes.

*Everyone's favorite.*

# COCONUT BARS

1/2 C brown sugar                     1/2 C butter
1 C flour


Blend together and pack in pan.  Bake 10 minutes, 350 degrees·
Mix the following and put on above after it is baked:

1 C brown sugar                    2 eggs, beaten
1/2 C walnuts                      2 Tbsp flour
1 1/2 C coconut                    1/4 tsp baking powder
1 tsp vanilla

Bake 20 minutes.

*Little kids don't like these because of the coconut and walnuts.*

# DATE SQUARES

3/4 C butter                       1/2 tsp soda
1 C brown sugar                    1 lb dates
1 1/2 C rolled oats                1/2 C sugar
1 1/2 C flour                      1/2 C water
1/4 tsp salt                       1 tsp lemon juice

Dice dates, add water, one-half cup sugar, and cook until mixture
is clear.  Add lemon juice and cool.  Sift flour once, add salt and
soda and sift together.  Cream butter and add sugar gradually.  Add
rolled oats and flour and mix well.  Place one half of mixture in
bottom of greased pan.  Spread with date filling and cover with
remainder of dough.  Bake and cut in squares while warm.  Bake
20 minutes at 350 degrees.

*Little kids won't eat these either.*

# DREAM BARS

1 C flour                          1/3 C brown sugar
1/2 C shortening (half butter)

Mix well with hands. Pat into pan 9 x 13 inches. Bake ten minutes. Spread over the following mixture:

| | |
|---|---|
| 2 well beaten eggs | 2 Tbsp flour |
| 1 1/4 C brown sugar | 3/4 C coconut |

Bake twenty minutes at 350 degrees. Cut into bars.

*Lean says, "Quick and easy".*

## ENGLISH TOFFEE

| | |
|---|---|
| 1/2 C butter | 1 C brown sugar |
| nuts - walnuts or pecans | |

Put butter and sugar in heavy sauce pan and cook 12 minutes, stirring constantly. Pour over a layer of nuts in buttered pie pan. Rub the surface with either bitter or sweet chocolate and shave a few nuts on top. When cold, break into small pieces.

*Favorite of Episcopalians.*

## LEMON BARS

Mix 2 cups flour and 1/2 C powdered sugar. Cut in 1 cup butter or margarine. Pat into a 9 x 13 inch pan. Bake 20 minutes at 350 degrees. Mix the following and spread over the first part:

| | |
|---|---|
| 2 C sugar | 1 tsp. baking powder |
| 4 eggs, slightly beaten | 4 Tbsp. lemon juice |
| 1 Tbsp. flour | |

Bake for 25 minutes longer. Cut into bars when cool.

## GUM DROP SQUARES

| | |
|---|---|
| 1 C. Crisco | 2 tsp. baking powder |
| 1 C brown sugar | 1/4 tsp. soda |
| 1/2 C. white sugar | 1 tsp. salt |
| 2 eggs and 1 yolk | 1/4 tsp. cloves |

1 tsp. vanilla
1/2 C. milk
2 C. flour

1/2 tsp. cinnamon
1 C. chopped gum drops
1 C. chopped walnuts

Cream Crisco and sugar. Add beaten eggs and vanilla. Add milk alternately with sifted dry ingredients. Add gum drops and nuts. Spread on 16 x 12 cookie sheet to bake. Dust with powdered sugar before serving. Bake for 30 minutes at 375°.

*A special treat to give to the confirmation age kids after they've got their memorization down to snuff.*

## HONEY DATE BARS

1 C. honey
1/2 C. shortening
3 eggs
1 tsp. vanilla
1 3/4 C. flour
1 tsp. baking powder

1 tsp. cinnamon
1/2 tsp. nutmeg
1 tsp. salt
1 C. chopped dates
1 C. chopped nuts

Cream honey and shortening. Add well beaten eggs and vanilla. Add sifted dry ingredients and beat until smooth. Add dates and nuts. Spread on cookie sheet 11 x 17 to bake. Cut in strips and roll in powdered sugar. Bake for 12 minutes at 375°.

*Some call these "Holy Land Bars".*

## MARBLED BROWNIES

1 C. butter
2 C. sugar
4 eggs
2 C. flour

1/2 tsp. salt
1 1/2 tsp. vanilla
2 C. chopped walnuts
2 squares chocolate

Cream butter and sugar. Add eggs one at a time, beating after each. Add flour, salt, vanilla and nuts. Divide batter into half and add melted chocolate to one half. Place batter by alternate spoonfuls in greased pan 8x8x2 inches and bake. Bake for 1 1/4 hour at 350 degrees.

*When your brown sugar is either gone or hard as a rock - make these.*

## MARSHMALLOW BARS

1/2 C. shortening (butter or margarine)
1 C. chunk peanut butter

2 - 6 oz. pkgs. Butterscotch or Toll House Morsels

Melt in double boiler and cool till nearly lukewarm.

Add and fold in:
3/4 C. flaked coconut
1 pkg. colored miniature marshmallows

1/2 C. nut meats may be added if using the cream style peanut butter

Cool and cut in squares. May be stored in refrigerator for an indefinite time. Use 13 x 9 inch pan.

## NUT GOODIES

1 C. sugar
1/2 C. butter
2 eggs
1 1/2 C. flour (scant)

1/2 tsp. vanilla
1 tsp. baking powder
1/2 C. chopped nuts

Cream sugar and butter. Add beaten eggs, flour, baking powder and vanilla. Spread on buttered pan and cover with nuts. Spread over it the following mixture:

1 C. brown sugar
2 egg whites

1/2 tsp. vanilla

Fold brown sugar and vanilla into beaten egg whites. Bake and cut in squares and remove from pan to cool. Bake for 30 minutes at 350 degrees.

*Good as "store bought" candy bars.*

## OATMEAL BARS

1 C. oatmeal                          1 1/4 C. boiling water

Stir and let stand for 20 minutes.

1/2 C. butter                         1 1/2 C. flour
1 C. brown sugar                      1 tsp. soda
1 C. white sugar                      1/4 tsp. salt
2 eggs                                1 tsp. vanilla

Cream butter and sugar; add eggs and vanilla; then add cooled oatmeal mixture and dry ingredients. Bake on a cookie sheet or 10x14 inch cake pan for 25 minutes at 350 degrees.

Topping
1/2 C. butter                         1 1/2 C. brown sugar
6 Tbsp. carnation milk or cream

Boil for 2 minutes, then add 1/2 C. nuts and 1 C. coconut. Beat and spread on while warm.

## ORANGE SLICE BARS

Mix 1/2 cup butter, 1/2 cup brown sugar, dash of salt and 1 cup flour. Press into a 9x13 inch ungreased pan. Bake 10 minutes at 375°. Then spread the following mixture over the bottom layer.

2 eggs, well beaten                   Dash of salt
1 C. brown sugar                      1 C. shredded coconut
1 tsp. vanilla                        1 C. cut up orange slices
2 Tbsp. flour                         1 C. nuts (optional)
1 tsp. baking powder

Bake for 25 minutes in 350 degrees oven.

*Make in winter when citrus fruit is in season.*

## PEANUT BUTTER BAR

1 C. white syrup                     2 C. sugar

Mix together until melted over burner. Shut off stove and add 1 cup peanut butter and mix well. Add 6 cups corn flakes (as they come from the box-do not crush). Put in greased 9x13 pan. Cut when cool.

*Easy as pie.*

## PRAYER BARS

First layer
5 Tbsp. cocoa                        1/4 C. butter

Melt over hot water and add:
1/2 C. powdered sugar
1 egg, slightly beaten               1 to 2 tsp. vanilla

Mix 2 cups crushed graham crackers, 1/2 C. nuts, 1 C. coconut. Add to first mixture and mix well. Press into 9x13 inch pan. Chill.

2nd layer
1/4 C. butter
3 Tbsp. cream                        1 tsp. vanilla

Melt and add 2 tsp. dry pudding mix. Remove from heat and add 2 cups powdered sugar. Blend well and spread over first layer.

3rd layer

1 3/4 oz. chocolate bar. Melt and spread over top. Bring to room temperature before cutting. Store in refrigerator.

*A favorite of Martin Luther.*

# SPICE BARS

| | |
|---|---|
| 1 C. brown sugar | 1 tsp. cloves |
| 3/4 C. shortening | 1 tsp. cinnamon |
| 2 eggs | 1/2 tsp. ginger |
| 1/2 C. molasses | 1/4 tsp. salt |
| 2 C. flour | 1 C. hot coffee |
| 1 tsp. soda | |

Bake at 325 degrees for 15 minutes. Frost.

*Sugar and spice and everything nice.*

## SUGARLESS BROWNIES

| | |
|---|---|
| 1 C. Karo syrup | 1 tsp. vanilla |
| 1/2 C. shortening | 1/2 tsp. baking powder |
| 2 squares chocolate | 1/4 tsp. salt |
| 3/4 C. flour | 1/2 C. chopped nut meats |
| 2 eggs | |

Beat together the syrup, shortening and melted chocolate. Sift flour, salt and baking powder. Add one-fourth cup of flour mixture, then the well beaten eggs and rest of flour. Spread on cookie sheet, and when baked, cover with the following frosting:

| | |
|---|---|
| 1 C. powdered sugar | 1 Tbsp. cocoa |
| 1 Tbsp. butter | 1 tsp. vanilla |
| 1 egg white | |

Beat together till creamy, and spread. Cut in squares. Bake for 35 minutes at 350 degrees.

*When you run out of sugar these are the tricks.*

## TUTTI FRUITI SQUARES

| | |
|---|---|
| 3/4 C. flour | 2 eggs |
| 1 C. chopped nuts | 1/2 tsp. salt |
| 3/4 C. sugar | 1 C. sliced dates |
| 1 tsp. baking powder | 3 Tbsp. melted fat |
| 1/4 C. each candied citron, | |

orange peel, cherries

Spread 3/4' thick in well greased shallow pan lined with wax paper. Bake in slow oven until firm to touch, about 3/4 to 1 hour.

*A fancy name for a fancy bar.*

## WALNUT STICKS

| | |
|---|---|
| 1/4 C. butter or Crisco | 1 egg |
| 1 C. light brown sugar | 1/2 C. black walnuts |
| 1 tsp. vanilla | 1 C. flour |
| 1/8 tsp. salt | 1 tsp. bakind powder |

Bake 30 minutes, makes 16 squares. 8 x 8 pan.

*Grown-up Bars.*

## WALNUT STRIPS

Crust
| | |
|---|---|
| 1/2 C. shortening | 1 C. flour |

Mix and pat into bottom of pan 8x14 inches. Bake 12 to 15 minutes.

Filling
| | |
|---|---|
| 2 eggs | 1/2 tsp. salt |
| 1 1/2 C. brown sugar | 1/2 C. chopped walnuts |
| 2 Tbsp. flour | 1/2 C. coconut (optional) |
| 1/4 tsp. baking powder | 1 tsp. vanilla |

Mix in order given and spread on crust. Return to oven and bake 15 to 20 minutes.

Frosting
| | |
|---|---|
| 2 Tbsp. butter | 2 Tbsp warm orange juice |
| 1 1/2 C. powdered sugar | 1 tsp. lemon juice |

Beat together till creamy and spread on cake. Cut in squares. Bake for 30 minutes at 350 degrees.

# CAKES

# CAKES

## BIBLE CAKES
### BIBLE CAKE

| | |
|---|---|
| 4 1/2 C. flour | 1 Kings 4:22 |
| 1 C. butter | Judges 5:22 (last clauses) |
| 2 C. sugar | Jeremiah 6:20 |
| 2 C. raisins | 1 Samuel 30:12 |
| 2 C. figs | Nahum 3:12 |
| 2 C. honey | 1 Samuel 14:25 |
| Pinch of salt | Leviticus 2:13 |
| 6 eggs | Jeremiah 17:11 |
| 1/2 C. Milk | Judges 4:19 (last clauses) |
| 2 cakes leaven | Amos 4:15 |
| Season to taste of spice | 11 Chronicles 9:19 |

*Some Lutheran church cookbooks call this Scripture Cake and make you look up the passages. We've saved you some work!*

# EVERYDAY CAKES

*These good old "stand-bys" are baked when you're under the gun,
on the run, with too much work that needs to be done."*

## APPLE UPSIDE-DOWN CAKE

2 eggs
1 C. flour
1 C. sugar
1 tsp. baking powder
1/4 tsp. salt

1/2 C. cold water
1 tsp. vanilla
3 to 4 apples pealed and
    sliced
1 C. sugar (for apples)
1 tsp. cinnamon

Beat eggs and beat the sugar into eggs. Sift flour once before
measuring and sift flour, baking powder and salt. Add to egg
mixture alternately with the water. Add vanilla. Bake in 9 inch
square pan, buttered and cover the bottom with sliced apples,
mixed with the 1 cup sugar and the cinnamon. Serve hot with
whipped cream.

*Make in the fall of the year when apples are plenty.*

## CRUMB CAKE

2 C. brown sugar
1/2 C. butter
2 C. flour
2 eggs

1 C. sour milk or
    buttermilk
1 tsp. soda
1 tsp. vanilla
1/2 C. nuts

Mix sugar, butter and flour together, as for pie crust. From this,
take out 3/4 cup of crumbs for frosting. Then add eggs, milk to
which soda has been added  Add vanilla and nuts, and beat for 10
minutes. Sprinkle remaining crumbs on unbaked cake. Bake in
loaf pan.

## SPICE CAKE

| | |
|---|---|
| 1 1/2 C. sugar | 3 tsp. baking powder |
| 1/2 C. shortening | 1/2 tsp. salt |
| 3 eggs | 1 tsp. cinnamon |
| 1 C. milk | 1/2 tsp. cloves |
| 1 tsp. vanilla | 1/2 tsp. nutmeg |
| 2 1/4 C. flour | 1/4 tsp. allspice |

Cream shortening, add sugar gradually. Beat egg yolks until lemon-colored, add to creamed mixture. Sift all dry ingredients, adding alternately with milk. Beat egg whites stiff and fold in last, together with vanilla. Bake at 350 degrees for 40 minutes if it's a loaf and 25 if it's a layer.

## VELVET LUNCH CAKE

| | |
|---|---|
| 1/2 C. butter | 2 C. flour, sifted with: |
| 1 C. brown sugar | 1 tsp. cinnamon |
| 1 C. sour milk | 1/4 tsp. cloves |
| 1 tsp. soda | 1/4 tsp. nutmeg |
| 1 egg | |

Cream shortening and sugar, add eggs. Beat thoroughly. Add flour and spices alternately with the sour milk. Bake in two greased 8 inch pans in moderate oven at 375°.

*Good for a man's lunch box.*

## RHUBARB CAKE

| | |
|---|---|
| 1 1/2 C. brown sugar | 1 egg |
| 1/2 C. shortening | 1/2 C. shortening |
| 1 C. sour milk or buttermilk | 1 tsp. soda |
| 2 C. flour | 1/4 tsp. salt |
| 1 tsp. vanilla | 1 1/2 C rhubarb (cut fine) |

Cream sugar and shortening. Beat in egg. Add rest of ingredients. Pour in pan (11x5x2). On top sprinkle 1/2 C. sugar mixed with 1/2 tsp. cinnamon. Bake at 350 degrees for 45 minutes. Serve with whipped cream or ice cream.

# FUNERAL CAKES

## CHERRY CAKE

3/4 C. shortening
1 1/2 C. sugar
1/2 tsp. vanilla
1/4 tsp. lemon extract
4 egg whites

1/2 C. finely chopped
   cherries
1 C. milk
3 C. cake flour
3 tsp. baking powder
1/4 tsp. salt

Cream shortening and sugar. Add flavoring and cherries, well drained. Alternate sifted dry ingredients with milk. Fold in well beaten egg whites. Pour in pan and bake.

## CHERRY COCONUT CAKE

1 C. flour
2 Tbsp. sugar

1/2 C. butter

Mix with fork and bake in moderate oven for ten minutes in 11 inch square pan.

Spread with following topping.

1 C. sugar
2 beaten eggs
1/4 C. flour
1/2 tsp. baking powder
Pinch of salt
1 tsp. vanilla

1 8-oz jar marachino
   cherries
1/2 of juice from jar
   of cherries
1 C. coconut

Bake in moderate oven about twenty minutes or until done.

## DEVILS FOOD CAKE

1 1/2 C. brown sugar
2 eggs
1/2 C. butter

2 C. sifted cake flour
1 tsp. soda
1/4 tsp. salt

3 squares chocolate (melted)         1 tsp. vanilla
1 C. sweet milk

Add soda and salt to flour and sift twice. Cream butter and sugar until light. Add eggs one at a time, beating well after each. Add melted chocolate. Alternately add flour with milk and vanilla. Bake at 325 degrees for 45 minutes in a 9x9 loaf pan.

## MAYONNAISE CAKE

1 C chopped nuts                3/4 C. mayonnaise (no
1 tsp. soda                        other dressing)
2 Tbsp. ground chocolate        1 C. boiling water
1 C. chopped dates              1 tsp. cinnamon
1 C. sugar                      1 tsp. vanilla
2 C. sugar                      2 C. flour

Mix soda and water, pour over dates and nuts. Let stand while mixing the other ingredients. Mix sugar, mayonnaise and vanilla, gradually adding flour, cinnamon and chocolate. Combine all and mix well. Bake in a moderate oven.

## MARBLE CAKE

WHITE PART
3 Tbsp shortening              1 C. flour
1/2 C. sugar                   2 tsp. baking powder
1/2 tsp. lemon extract         1/4 tsp. salt
1/2 C. milk                    white of one egg

DARK PART
3 Tbsp. shortening             1/4 tsp. salt
1/2 C. sugar                   1/2 tsp. cloves
yolk of one egg                1/2 tsp. nutmeg
1/2 C. milk                    1 tsp. cinnamon
1 C. flour                     2 Tbsp. cocoa
2 tsp. baking powder

Use 2 bowls - Part 1: Cream shortening, add sugar slowly, add flavoring and milk. Beat well, and add flour sifted with salt and baking powder. Fold in beaten egg white. Part 2: Cream shortening, add sugar slowly then egg yolk and mix well. Add

89

milk, and flour with baking powder, salt, spice and cocoa, which have been sifted together. Put both batters by spoonfuls alternately into greased pans, but do not mix. Bake in moderate oven about 45 minutes. Cover with white icing.

## MARBLE COCOA CAKE

2 C. of flour (sifted five times)  
1 C. sugar  
1/2 C. butter  

3 egg whites  
1 C. milk  
1/2 tsp. vanilla  
1/2 tsp. baking powder

Cream butter and sugar. Sift baking powder and flour, and add milk alternately with flour. Add flavoring and beaten egg whites. Separate the batter and to one-half of it add; three teaspoons of cocoa, one half teaspoon each of nutmeg, allspice and cinnamon, and 1/4 teaspoon of soda. Beat well and drop in buttered pan, first one teaspoon of white batter and then a spoonful of dark until used up.

## ORANGE CAKE

1 C. sugar  
1/2 C. shortening  
1 C. sweet milk  
2 eggs  
juice of 1 orange  
rind of 1/2 orange  

2 C. flour  
1 tsp. soda  
1 tsp. baking powder  
1/8 tsp. salt  
1 C. raisins

Cream sugar, shortening and orange rind. Add well beaten eggs. Sift flour, soda, baking powder and salt. Grind or cut up raisins, dredge with 1/4 cup of the flour. Add dry and liquid ingredients to creamed mixture; add raisins last. Bake at 350 degrees in a 9x9 loaf pan for 45 minutes.

## PRUNE CAKE

1/2 C. butter  
1 C. sugar  
2 eggs  
1 tsp. cinnamon  

1/2 tsp. cloves  
1 C. cut up prunes (cook  
   before) - no juice  
1 C. buttermilk with 1

1 tsp. vanilla                          tsp. soda
                                        2 C. sifted cake flour

Cream butter and sugar.  Add remaining ingredients.  Bake 30 minutes at 350 degrees.  Frost with white icing (recipe elsewhere in chapter) and cut in 4" pieces.

*Good for funerals.*

## WATKINS CHOCOLATE DESSERT CAKE

| | |
|---|---|
| 1 C. sugar and 2 Tbsp shortening creamed together | 1/2 C. Watkins Chocolate |
| 1 egg | 1/4 tsp. salt |
| 1 1/2 C. flour | 2 tsp. Watkins Baking Powder |

Break egg into cup, fill with milk and beat, add sugar and shortening.  Sift flour, salt, Watkins Chocolate Dessert and baking powder together, add to first mixture, then add 1 tsp. Watkins Vanilla.  Bake in layers, 375° F. oven, 25 minutes. Use your favorite frosting.

## BASIC ICING RECIPES

### WHITE ICING

1 C. sugar                              1/2 C. water
2 egg whites beaten stiffly             1 tsp. vanilla

Cook the sugar and water in a small saucepan until it spins a thread.  Pour the sugar and water mixture into the beaten egg whites and beat until glossy.  Add vanilla and beat again.  Spread on cake.

### CHOCOLATE ICING

1 C. powdered sugar                     1/3 square chocolate
2 Tbsp. milk or cream

Melt chocolate, add to sugar and moisten with liquid.

# LADIES AID CAKES
## Always Bring Your Best!!

### CHOCOLATE MOCHA CAKE

1 egg
1 C. sugar
1/2 C. butter
1 C. sour milk
1 tsp. soda

1 1/2 C. flour
2 Tbsp. cocoa
1 tsp. vanilla
2 tsp. baking powder

Cream butter, add sugar, then eggs and beat until light. Add soda and cocoa then sour milk. Work in flour with baking powder and beat 100 times. Bake in slow oven.

### CREAM CAKE

1 C. sugar
1/3 C. sweet cream
4 eggs, well beaten
1/8 tsp. salt

1 1/4 C. cake flour
2 tsp. baking powder
1 tsp. lemon flavoring

Sift flour, measure and sift with baking powder and salt. Combine sugar, eggs and cream. Stir until well blended. Add flavoring. Add dry ingredients. Beat five minutes. Pour into well oiled shallow pan. Bake in 375° oven 30 minutes.

### DAFFODIL CAKE

1 C. cake flour
1/2 C. sugar
1 1/3 C. egg whites
1/4 tsp. salt
1 1/4 tsp. cream of tartar
1 C. sugar

1 tsp. vanilla
1/2 tsp. almond extract
4 well beaten egg yolks
2 Tbsp. cake flour
1 tsp. lemon extract
1 tsp. vanilla

Sift 1 cup flour with 1/2 cup sugar three times. Beat egg whites until frothy. Add salt and cream of tartar, beat until stiff, but still glossy. Add the 1 cup sugar gradually. Add vanilla and lemon extract. Fold in flour mixture gradually. Divide the batter in two parts. In one half fold egg yolks, 2 Tbsp. flour and lemon extract. Fold vanilla into other half. Spoon batter alternately into 10 inch ungreased angel pan. Bake at 325 degrees for 1 hour.

*A good cake to serve at Spring Ladies Aid Banquet. Some plastic daffodil and tulip centerpieces would make a good compliment to this cake.*

## GOLD CAKE

1 1/2 C sugar
1 1/4 C. flour
1/2 C water
6 eggs beaten separately
1/4 tsp. salt

1 C cake flour
3/4 tsp. cream of tartar
1 tsp lemon or orange
   extract

Boil sugar and water until it threads when dropped from tip of spoon. Pour the hot syrup in a fine stream over the beaten egg whites to which salt has been added, beating mixture until cool. Then add the well beaten egg yolks. Sift the flour once, measure, add cream of tartar and sift again three times. Fold carefully into egg mixture. Add extract. Pour into ungreased angel cake pan and bake 50-60 minutes in moderately slow oven (325-350 degrees F.) When done invert to cool.

## LADY BALTIMORE CAKE

1/2 C. butter (cream butter
   and sugar
1 C. milk
1 1/3 C. sugar

1/2 C. sifted cake flour
vanilla flavor
lastly 4 well beaten egg
   whites

FILLING FOR CAKE:
6 Tbsp. sugar
2 Tbsp corn starch
1 lemon (grated)

1/2 C. cold water
4 egg yolks
salt

Cook in double boiler and when cool spread between layers of cake. A white frosting on top and over all makes a fine party finish.

# OLD FASHIONED JELLY ROLL

3/4 C. sifted cake flour
3/4 tsp. baking powder
3/4 C. sugar
1/4 tsp. salt

4 eggs
1 tsp. vanilla
1 C. jelly (any flavor)

Sift flour once, measure. Combine baking powder, salt and eggs in bowl. Place over small bowl of hot water and beat with rotary beater, adding sugar gradually until mixture becomes thick and light colored. Remove bowl from hot water. Fold in flour and vanilla. Turn into greased pan, 15x10 inches lined with greased paper and bake at 400 degrees for 13 minutes. Quickly cut off crisp edges of cake. Turn from pan at once onto cloth covered with powdered sugar. Remove paper. Spread with jelly, almost to edge. Roll quickly. Wrap in cloth and cool on rack.

# RICH WHITE CAKE

1 1/4 C. sugar

1/2 C. butter

Cream.

1/2 C. milk
3 egg whites beaten

2 C. flour
2 tsp. baking powder

Sift flour and baking powder together three times. Flavor with lemon juice and vanilla.

# SPRING BEAUTY CAKE

1 C. sifted cake flour
1 tsp. baking powder
1/4 tsp. salt
1 C. sugar

2 tsp. lemon juice
6 Tbsp. hot milk
3 eggs

Sift flour, baking powder and salt together three times. Beat eggs with rotary egg beaten until thick enough to stand up in soft peaks (5 to 7 minutes). Add sugar gradually, beating constantly. Add lemon juice. Fold in flour, a small amount at a time. Add hot milk and stir quickly until thoroughly blended. Turn at once into an ungreased tube pan and bake in moderate oven (350 degrees) 35 minutes or until done. Remove from pan and invert pan 1 hour or until cold. Remove from pan and pile strawberry fluff topping on top of cake.

## STRAWBERRY FLUFF FROSTING

Combine 1 egg white, unbeaten, 1/2 cup sugar, dash of salt and 1/3 cup sliced strawberries in top of double boiler and beat with rotary egg beater until thoroughly mixed. Place over rapidly boiling water, beat constantly with rotary beater and cook three minutes, or until mixer will stand in soft peaks. Remove from heat and fold in 1/3 cup sliced strawberries.

## SNOW CAKE

| | |
|---|---|
| 1/4 C. butter | 1 2/3 C. flour |
| 1 C. white sugar | 1 rounding tsp. baking |
| 2 egg whites | powder |
| 1/2 C. milk | 1/2 tsp. vanilla |

Cream butter, sugar and vanilla. Beat egg whites to stiff froth. Sift flour and baking powder thoroughly. Add to first mixture and lastly fold in egg whites. Cover with boiled icing.

# ANGEL FOOD CAKES

## ANGEL FOOD CAKE

| | |
|---|---|
| 12 egg whites, very cold | 1 1/8 C. cake flour |
| 1 1/2 C. sugar | 1-16 tsp. salt |
| 1 tsp. cream of tartar | 1/2 tsp. any flavoring |

Sift and measure sugar and flour separately and sift each four more times. Add salt to egg whites and beat until foamy. Add cream of tartar and beat until egg whites hold their shape when bowl is inverted. Add sugar slowly folding in, add flavoring and fold in flour carefully. Baking time is 50 minutes, put in slow oven (150 degrees) and increase heat gradually until last 15 minutes are 350 degrees.

## CHOCOLATE ANGEL FOOD CAKE

1 1/2 C. egg whites
1 1/2 C. sugar, sifted
3/4 C. sifted cake flour
1/4 C. cocoa

1 tsp. cream of tartar
1/8 tsp. salt
1 1/2 tsp. vanilla

Add salt to egg whites, beat until foamy, add cream of tartar and beat until whites will hang to beater. Then fold in sugar slowly - in the same manner as in making mush, by taking handfuls and letting it sift slowly through the fingers. Add flavoring - then fold for 30 minutes, then 310 degrees for 30 minutes, or until done.

## ORANGE ANGEL FOOD CAKE

1 1/2 C. sifted sugar
1 1/2 C. sifted cake flour
8 eggs
grated rind of 1 orange

1/2 tsp. cream of tartar
1/3 C. orange juice
1 1/2 tsp. vanilla
1/2 tsp. lemon juice

Beat yolks until lemon-colored; add three-fourths of the sugar gradually, rind, juice and flavoring. Beat egg whites as for angel food. Add cream of tartar when frothy. Add rest of sugar gradually to whites. Fold in egg yolk mixture, then fold in flour, which has been sifted before measuring and sifted several times after measuring. Bake at 350 degrees for 1 hour.

## MOCK ANGEL FOOD CAKE

1 1/2 C. sugar
2 C. cake flour
1 C. boiling water
1/2 tsp. vanilla

5 egg whites
1/4 tsp. salt
1 tsp. cream of tartar
2 tsp. baking powder

First mix sugar and flour after sifting once. Into this, pour the boiling water while stirring well. Let it cool before starting the rest. Then, beat egg whites with salt and cream of tartar until they hold a point or will not fall out, when tipped upside down. Next sprinkle the baking powder on whites and beat a little.

Then pour very slowly, the heavy mixture into rest, and fold in very carefully. Bake in loaf or layer with heat as for other cake.

## YELLOW ANGEL FOOD

3 egg yolks
1 C. sugar
7 Tbsp. cold water
1 tsp. vanilla

1 C. cake flour
1 tsp. baking powder
pinch of salt
3 egg whites

Beat the egg yolks until lemon color, then add sugar and beat until good and light. Add cold water, vanilla and beat again. Sift flour, baking powder and salt together and add to batter. Beat well. Beat egg whites stiff and fold in lightly. Bake in moderate oven.

# SPONGE CAKES

## ANGEL SPONGE CAKE

4 eggs
2 C. sugar
1 C. boiling water

2 C. cake flour
2 tsp. baking powder
1/2 tsp. cream of tartar

Beat eggs for five minutes, add sugar and beat thoroughly. Add the boiling water, then the flour containing baking powder and cream of tartar. Flavor to suit taste and bake in an ungreased pan about 40 minutes. This makes a large cake.

## HOT MILK SPONGE CAKE

1 C. sugar
1 Tbsp. butter
1/2 C. boiling hot milk
1/4 tsp. almond flavoring
1 tsp. vanilla

2 eggs
1/4 tsp. salt
1 tsp. baking powder
1 C. sifted Gold Medal
Flour

Beat eggs and salt until very light. Beat in sugar and flavoring, add butter to boiling milk, then add flour sifted with baking powder. Bake at once in an 8 inch square pan for 25 minutes at

325 degrees. Cut in strips. Roll in powdered sugar. This should be made with a dover of electric mixer.

## SPEEDY SPONGE CAKE

2 eggs
1 C. sugar
1 C. enriched flour
1/8 tsp. salt

1 tsp. baking powder
1 Tbsp. butter
1/2 C. hot milk

Beat eggs until light and thick. Slowly add sugar and beat with a spoon 5 minutes or with electric mixer 2 1/2 minutes. Fold sifted dry ingredients into egg and sugar mixture all at once. Melt butter in hot milk and add all at once. The folding-in of the dry ingredients and milk should take only one minute. Bake in wax paper lines 8-inch square pan in moderate oven (350 degrees) for 30 minutes.

## BAKED-ON-FROSTING

Beat 1 egg white with 1/4 tsp. baking powder. Gradually beat in 1/2 cup brown sugar; spread over hot cake. Sprinkle with 1/4 cup chopped nut meats. Bake in moderate oven (350 degrees) until lightly browned and bubbly (about 15 minutes).

## ORANGE SPONGE CAKE

5 eggs
1/2 tsp. cream of tartar
1 1/2 C. sugar (sifted)
3 tsp. grated orange rind

1/2 C. orange juice
1/2 tsp. salt
1 3/4 C. cake flour
2 1/4 tsp. baking powder

Beat egg whites and cream of tartar until stiff. Add well beaten egg yolks and sugar. Add flour sifted with baking powder and salt, and orange juice. Bake in 3 8-inch layer pans. Fill with rich lemon filling and frost with 3 minute frosting.

## SPONGE CAKE

10 egg yolks
1 C. sugar
1/2 C. cold water

1 tsp. lemon extract
1 1/2 C. cake flour
1 tsp. baking powder

1/8 tsp. salt

Place egg yolks, sugar and water in mixer and beat for 15 minutes at medium speed. Then sift four times the cake flour, salt and baking powder. Fold into egg yolk mixture and add lemon extract. Bake 1 hour at 325 degrees.

## WHIPPED CREAM CAKE

| | |
|---|---|
| 1 C. sweet cream | 2 C. cake flour |
| 3 egg whites | 3 tsp. baking powder |
| 1/2 C. water | 1/2 tsp. salt |
| 1 tsp. vanilla | 1 1/2 C. sugar |

Whip cream after measuring, beat egg whites stiff, combine with cream, add water and vanilla. Sift together flour, baking powder, salt and sugar (flour and sugar having been sifted separately several times). Gradually fold in dry ingredients into egg mixture a little at a time. Bake at 375 degrees for 30 minutes in a 9 inch layer pan.

# SVEA JOHNSON'S UGLY CAKE

HISTORY: Mrs. Johnson was an elderly widow, who made this delicious cake from apples her tree bore every fall. Though it was not expected of her, she always wanted to do her part in providing for the church suppers, so she brought her "Comfort Cake". Since it was not frosted, it was relegated to a position in the back at the end of the serving table. That is where we young ones discovered it, laid claim and enjoyed two and three helpings. it was referred quietly by the committee, as "Mrs. Johnson's Ugly Cake". We watched for that cake and had little competition because it was so unassuming.

One year a committee member told Mrs. Johnson she would come by and pick up the cake to make it easier for her; which she did. She took it home and covered it with a sour cream icing; then the cake became acceptable, others learned of the taste, and we lost our claim to Mrs. Johnson's Ugly Cake.

We paid a visit to Mrs. Johnson and asked for the recipe, which pleased her mightily. Whenever I make this cake, it brings back memories, and while the frosting is delicious, I never frost it, because it is so good in its unassuming state. (1930's)

## SVEA JOHNSON'S COMFORT CAKE

| | |
|---|---|
| 2 C. sugar | 1 tsp. salt |
| 3 C. flour | 2 tsp. cinnamon |
| 1 tsp. baking soda | |

Mix above ingredients in a large bowl then add:

| | |
|---|---|
| 1 1/3 C. melted shortening | 2 eggs |
| (I now use salad oil) | 2 tsp. vanilla |

Stir together and then add:

| | |
|---|---|
| 4 C. peeled, chopped apples | 1/2 C. raisins |

Pour batter into greased 9x13 pan and bake for 1/2 hours as 325 degrees (her way) or 1 hour at 350 degrees (my way) till cake leaves sides of pan. The cake is moist and will keep for a long time if no one discovers it; if they do-- it's a "flash in the pan".

## SOUR CREAM FROSTING

1 C. sour cream                    3 or 4 egg yolks
1 C. sugar

Cook until thickened then spread on cake and sprinkle with chopped nuts. (This is the frosting that spoiled our claim to the Ugly Cake and put it on the plates of the multitude).

# FRUIT CAKES

Lovely to look at, lovely to behold,
bought at bazaars, they're always marked sold.

Chucked full of citron, they're heavy as gold,
but no one will eat them is what we've been told.

Forsaken and lonely, they turn stale and old,
they sit on a shelf till they dry up and mold.

# FRUITCAKES

Making and serving fruitcake at Christmas is not a unique Lutheran experience. In fact, Lutheran women rarely serve fruitcake at church functions. We are told that Christians from other cultures and religious persuasions are also caught up in this habit. "Why?" you ask. We can only guess. Maybe it's because some of the main ingredients found in fruitcakes - dates, nuts, citron, and raisins, - remind Lutherans and other Christians of the Holy Lands. Maybe fruitcakes are something Lutherans and other Christians know they'll always have on hand just in case they're caught shorthanded without much to serve if someone drops by to visit; or maybe it's just a tradition that all Christians have learned to respect, but never question. Consequently, we felt a Lutheran obligation to put fruitcakes recipes in this church cookbook.

## DARK FRUITCAKE

| | |
|---|---|
| 2 lbs raisins (chopped) | 1 lb citron (cut up) |
| 2 lbs currants (washed & dried) | 12 eggs |
| 1 lb flour | 1 lb sugar |
| 3 Tbsp grated nutmeg | 1 Tbsp mace |
| 1 1/2 Tbsp cinnamon | 1 lb butter |
| * 1 lg tumbler wine or fruit juice | |

Beat butter and sugar to a cream. Beat eggs without separating until light and creamy. Add to butter and sugar, mix in flour, with which spices have been sifted. Cut, wash and dry fruit and dredge with 1/2 cup flour and stir into cake. Take an extra large tumbler of wine or fruit juice and stir into cake last. Turn mixture into a well greased pan and bake 3 hours - 250 degrees F. I like to steam this cake 3 hours then bake it 1 1/2 hours at 250 degrees F.

*Don't use wine if there is a chance you might be bringing this to church.*

# FRUITCAKE

1 C sugar
3/4 C Crisco or butter
3 C sifted flour
4 eggs
1/2 C molasses
1/2 lb chopped dates
1 lb currants
1/4 lb candied lemon peel
1/4 lb candied orange peel
1/4 lb citron

1/4 C jelly
1/2 C fruit juice or sour
   milk
1 tsp soda
1 tsp salt
1/2 tsp cloves
1/2 tsp cinnamon
1/2 tsp allspice
1/4 lb candied pineapple
1/4 lb candied red cherries
1/4 lb candied green
   cherries

Cream shortening and sugar, add eggs one at a time, beating well after each egg is added. Sift together the flour, soda, salt and spices, and add alternately with jelly, molasses and fruit juice, or sour milk (all blended together). Add the nuts and chopped fruits which have been slightly floured. This may be baked in one-pound (low style) coffee cans or in small loaf pans. If pans are lined with wax paper, cake will keep fresh longer.


# MINCE MEAT FRUITCAKE

1 lb mince meat
1 C raisins
1 C chopped nuts
1 C chopped glazed fruit
2 C all purpose flour
1 1/2 tsp baking powder

1/2 tsp soda
1 C sugar
1/2 C melted shortening
1 tsp vanilla
2 eggs, separated

To the mince meat, add raisins, nutmeats and chopped fruit. Cream sugar and shortening, add egg yolks and beat thoroughly. Sift flour, baking powder, soda and salt together once, and then sift and fold into mince meat mixture. Fold in stiffly beaten egg whites and vanilla. Grease pan well. Bake in a tube cake pan for 1 1/2 hours.

# STEAMED FRUITCAKE

2 C shortening
2 2/3 C lt brown sugar
9 eggs
1/2 C molasses
1/2 C strong coffee infusion
1/2 C grape or fruit juice
1 Tbsp vanilla
1/2 tsp soda
5 1/2 C all purpose flour
3 tsp baking powder
1 Tbsp cloves
1 tsp salt

2 lbs raisins, chopped
1 1/2 lbs of currants
1/2 lb of candied cherries
1/4 lb of citron, cut fine
1/4 lb lemon peel, cut fine
1/4 lb orange peel, cut fine
2 C blanched & chopped almonds
2 Tbsp cinnamon
1 Tbsp nutmeg

Cream the shortening and sugar together. Beat the eggs and add, stirring until well mixed. Add the molasses, coffee, fruit juice, and vanilla. Dissolve the soda in a tablespoonful of hot water in the coffee, then add to the mixture and stir. Sift the flour, measure the correct amount, reserve 1 cupful for dredging the fruit, and sift the remaining flour with the baking powder, spices, and salt. Add the flour to the above mixture and beat. Add the fruit and almonds, dredged with flour, and stir until thoroughly mixed. Pour into 2 large or several small loaf pans lined with wax paper. Whole almonds and candied cherries may be arranged on the tops of the cakes. Place in a steamer and steam 3 hours. Remove to a slow oven (300 degrees) and bake for 1 hour. Cool and store to ripen.

# WHITE FRUITCAKE

1 C butter
2 C sugar
6 egg whites
1 C coconut
1 C nuts
4 C flour
3 tsp baking powder
1 C sweet milk

Pinch of salt
1 tsp vanilla
1/2 C each: citron,
    orange & lemon peel
1 bottle cherries with juice
1 lg Cup white raisins
1 lg Cup dates (cut up)

Cream sugar and butter. Add milk and cherry juice alternately with sifted dry ingredients with exception of 1 cup flour used to flour fruits and nuts. Add these after the milk and flour. Add extract and salt. Fold in stiffly beaten whites last. Bake one hour.

*This one looks Norwegian!*

# LUTHERAN CHURCH
# BASEMENT WOMEN

# LUTHERAN CHURCH
# BASEMENT WOMEN

### TWENTY STATEMENTS THAT LUTHERAN WOMEN CAN'T SAY, BUT AT THE WRONG TIME OF THE MONTH MIGHT THINK (Not Christian)

1. That's the fourth time she has used that excuse.
2. They are dying likes flies around here. If I have to bring another cake I think I will scream.
3. Don't call me for anything. I'm too busy.
4. Get some of the younger ones to do it.
5. If we run out, that's just too bad.
6. I don't want to listen to your complaints. I have enough trouble of my own.
7. Tell her to cater it!
8. It's about time we started using paper cups.
9. She hasn't been in church for ages, then shows up for the banquet. Figures.
10. I don't know how she dares to ask us to serve.
11. We're not a restaurant for crying out loud.
12. I can't work. (no explanation).
13. Who does she think she is anyway?
14. What do we have a janitor for anyway?
15. I haven't seen the pastor's wife get her hands in a sink of water.
16. Nobody needs a big meal for a 3 o'clock funeral, that's for sure. Sandwiches will just have to do.
17. Life's not a bowl of cherries for anyone.
18. She isn't the only one who has got other commitments.
19. Let's keep it simple.
20. Why do Lutherans think they have to eat every time they go to church?

## TWENTY STATEMENTS HEARD BY PROPER, CHEERFUL LUTHERAN WOMEN (Christian)

1. It's nothing.

2. I'm sorry.

3. You sit down and let me do it.

4. I will be more than happy to help.

5. What can I bring then?

6. Don't think a thing about it.

7. I'll stand. I've been sitting all morning.

8. Mange tusen tak.

9. Give me the dishtowel. It's my turn now.

10. You've had a long day. Sit down then.

11. I haven't had my turn.

12. I have nothing better to do.

13. I can easily double the recipe.

14. It's ing a ting.

15. Keep the dishes coming.

16. Give me the dishtowels. I'm washing tomorrow anyway.

17. I'm not helpless.

18. I can be there by 6 in the morning.

19. It's about time I return the favor.

20. Keep me posted. I can get there in a flash.

# TYPES OF LUTHERAN CHURCH BASEMENT WOMEN

| Mary Types - The Listeners | Martha Types - The Doers |
|---|---|
| 1. Gives devotions | 1. Organizes kitchen crew |
| 2. Serves coffee | 2. Makes coffee |
| 3. Arranges centerpiece | 3. Sets and cleans tables |
| 4. High heel shoes and nylons | 4. Wedges and anklets |
| 5. Fancy aprons | 5. Everyday or catch-all apron |
| 6. Introduces speaker | 6. Serves speaker |
| 7. Plays piano | 7. Dusts piano |
| 8. Visit with speaker | 8. Washes dishes |
| 9. Arranges for next speaker | 9. Takes down tables & cleans up. |
| 10. Announces meeting | 10. Serves next meeting |

## LUTHERAN LADIES AID ETIQUETTE

1. Be a cheerful giver. Give food, money, and time whenever called upon.

2. Be an officer. Even if you are shy, there's something you can do.

3. When the Ladies Aid president calls for a cake for a funeral, don't be skimpy. Use your biggest pan. Remember, funeral cake is cut into 4 inch squares.

4. If someone gives you a compliment on the food you prepared, a proper response would be - It wasn't much then. Keep it humble and nobody will think you are a show off.

5. Always bring more food than what is asked of you, so other people won't think you are cheap and skimpy.

## TIMES TO BRING FOOD TO THE PASTOR

1. Day of arrival
2. Christmas - bring your Sunday best. (Mark down the cost. This can be counted towards your tithe).
3. When someone is the pastor's family is sick.
4. When the pastor's wife has a baby.
5. Easter
6. When the pastor leaves - if he leaves in good standing.

## LUTHERAN MEASUREMENTS - RULES OF THUMB

Time - Cook until done. It's just got that certain look.

A Little Bit - A couple of pinches, but go easy then.

Pinch - Not too much. (Wash hands before you do this).

A lot - Make sure you have enough flour for this one.

Flour To Roll - Don't run out of flour. It could get to be a sticky situation.

Ing A Ting - A little less than a 1/2 pinch. If you don't have the ingredient, it won't matter anyway.

Lunch For A Bunch - Always count on extras, you just never know. It is better to have enough than to run out.

Temperature Tester - Spit will sizzle when the pan is hot enough.

Recipe Stretching - Add water or flour depending upon the situation.

If no baking temperature is given, 350 degrees is reliable as the noon whistle.

# WOMEN'S APRONS

## *The Basic Six*

1. Serving Apron

   This is the "Lutheran Standard" of all aprons. Most Lutheran women who are willing workers and willing servers own several of theses 24 inch long, slightly pressed, gathered and tied at the waist, flowered or gingham-checked, cotton serving aprons. Adorned with only one handy pocket, these aprons are not used for heavy duty serving.

2. Anniversary Apron

   This apron is worn by Lutheran women who serve Silver and Golden wedding anniversaries in the church basement. Most people who aren't Lutheran can't tell the difference between this apron and a serving apron. Lutheran women can. The anniversary apron is usually fancier. The gingham-checked aprons usually have some cross-stitch running across the bottom of the apron, and the flowered ones have a couple of rows of ric-rac or trim on them to dress them up a little bit.

3. Wedding Apron

   Lutheran brides purchase these little, white, lacy and see-through (not risqué though), stiff, organza aprons for friends and family members who serve coffee at their wedding. Given as a gift to the wedding coffee servers, they're usually put in a closet and never used again. They're impractical and a waste of good money, but they are necessary and appropriate attire for coffee servers at Lutheran weddings.

4.  Catch-All Apron

Because they cover Lutheran servers from the shoulders to
the knees, this all-purpose, understated apron is a favorite for
Lutheran women when they're "heavy duty" serving. (Heavy
duty serving takes place at annual lutefisk suppers.)  Some
Lutheran men* wear them when they're cooking for mother-
daughter banquets.  Loaded with pockets, they're practical but
not pretty.  In Lutheran homes these aprons are usually hung
up and not folded in drawers.

* Lutheran mem wear only white aprons.


5.  The Everday Apron

(Some pronounce it everday).  These are the worn out
serving and catch-all aprons that Lutheran women wear
around their homes and only wear in church when they're
doing the annual spring and fall cleaning of the church
basement kitchen.


6.  Dishtowel Apron

Another apron worn by both Lutheran women and Lutheran
men.  Lutheran women wear them in a pinch when for some
reason or another they forget their appropriate apron at home;
but Lutheran men who do dishes at mother-daughter banquets
use them without thinking a thing about it.  Some
Lutherans throw them over their shoulder when cooking so
they have something to wipe their hand on, or they use them
as potholders when the unexpected comes up.

Footnote: The young Mrs. Ole Johnson doesn't always get her wash done on Mondays, and her neighbor said she's seen her use a dishtowel as a diaper. Ish da. Then others said they weren't surprised because the mother of the young Mrs. Ole Johnson once wore a dishtowel over her head to church, took it off, and went into the church kitchen and started drying dishes with it. People talked about it for years and years. As Lena Larson said "Train up a child . . . ".

# SAFE AND PROPER KNOTS
## USED FOR TYING
## LUTHERAN CHURCH BASEMENT
## WOMEN'S DISHTOWELS

### For Aprons

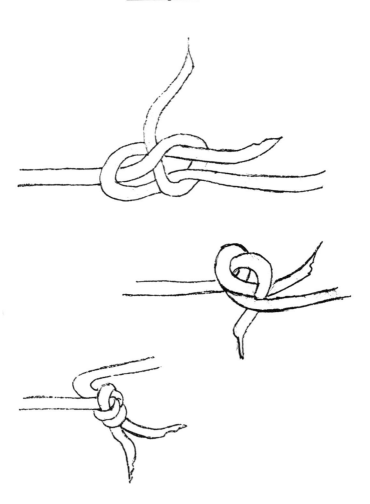

## For Scarves

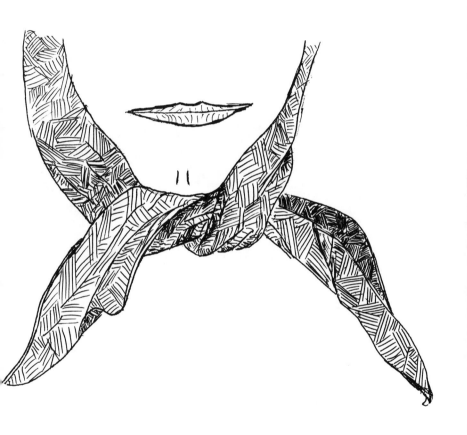

## For   Hotdishes

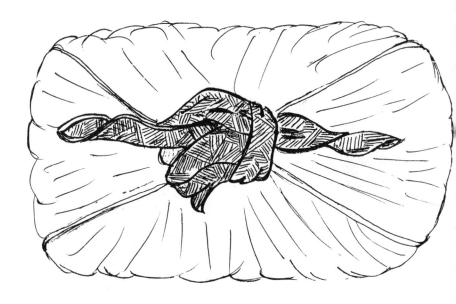

# BETWEEN THE NINE
## AND ELEVEN

# BETWEEN THE
# NINE AND ELEVEN

Non-Lutherans, heathens, and liberal psychologists are puzzled why Lutherans have to be served a little lunch between the 9 and 11 o'clock services. Some argue it's heredity, others say it's environmental, and the cynics say it's just a habit.

Ole Axelson, a baptized and confirmed Lutheran can't understand what the fuss is all about. "That's nothing to get excited about," he said. "The mind hears the words 'vaer sa god', and the stomach says it's time for lunch. It's as easy as that." Lena, his wife, says it's Biblical. "Jesus stopped his services so his disciples could gather fish and bread for everyone to eat. If it was good enough for the Lord, it's good enough for me," she said.

## COFFEE FOR SIXTY

| 1 pound coffee | 12 quarts water |
|---|---|

Put coffee into cloth bag large enough so that the coffee after swelling will be held loosely in the bag. Drop bag into boiling water. Boil for five to eight minutes, then remove bag. One quart of cream will serve sixty people.

*Some made egg coffee depending upon who was serving*

## WATKIN NECTAR AND KOOL-AID

This was for the kids or visitors who didn't drink coffee. Sometimes only water was served.

## BROWN SUGAR COOKIES

| 2 eggs | 2 tsp cream tartar |
|---|---|
| 1 1/3 C brown sugar | 1 tsp soda |
| 2/3 C butter and lard (in equal parts) | 1/4 tsp salt |
| | 3 C flour (rounding) |
| 1 tsp vanilla | |

Combine sugar, butter and eggs well beaten. Add flour, soda, cream of tartar and salt, mixed and sifted together, then vanilla. Roll thin and shape with a small cutter. Bake in a hot oven.

*Three cups of flour is certainly different than three cups of flour (rounding). Lutheran Church Basement Women know the difference, do you?*

## BUTTER COOKIES

| | |
|---|---|
| 1 C butter | 2 1/4 C flour (sifted) |
| 1 C granulated sugar | 1/2 tsp soda |
| 1 tsp Watkins Cream of Tartar | 1/2 tsp Watkins Vanilla |
| 2 eggs | 1/2 tsp Watkins Lemon Extract |

Cream butter, add sugar and beat well. Add beaten eggs, then sifted dry ingredients. Chill dough. Roll thin on lightly floured board. Cut, sprinkle with sugar, decorate with bits of candied cherries. Bake on greased cookie sheet 8 to 10 minutes in 375° F. Keep in covered tin. The less flour used, the more crisp the cookies.

*Some cooks cheapen this cookie up by using lard. No one will say anything but everyone will know it. What could be worse then?*

## EXCELLENT WHITE COOKIES

| | |
|---|---|
| 3 eggs | 1/2 C sweet milk |
| 2 C sugar | 1 tsp soda |
| 1/2 C butter | 1/2 tsp baking powder |
| 1/2 C lard | Flour to mix for rolling |

Beat shortening, add sugar and yolks. Beat well. Add baking powder and soda to part of flour, add milk, whites of eggs, and remaining flour. Roll out the dough very thin. Bake in a quick oven.

*This recipe states that the cookies should be baked in a "quick oven". Only veteran cooks should try this recipe because they're the only ones who know what it means to bake cookies in a "quick oven".*

## MOLASSES COOKIES

3/4 C shortening
1 C white sugar
1 egg (beaten)
4 Tbsp molasses
2 tsp soda

1/4 tsp salt
2 C flour and 2 or 3 Tbsp
   more if necessary
1 tsp ginger
1 tsp cinnamon
1/2 tsp cloves

Mix and form in balls. Roll in sugar and bake.

*This recipe calls for 2 cups of flour and 2 or 3 tablespoons more if necessary. Beware of this recipe if you don't have enough cooking sense to know how to feel dough.*

## PEANUT BUTTER COOKIES

1 C brown sugar
1/2 C butter
1/2 C peanut butter
1 1/2 C flour

1 tsp soda
vanilla
pinch of salt

Mix ingredients in the order given. Form in small balls on cookie sheet and press down with fork. Bake in oven at 350 degrees.

*Not a dunker, but a hit with kids. Sometimes they get dry and stick to the roof of your mouth. Don't eat it if you have a habit of gagging or a condition that causes you to clear your throat.*

## SALTED PEANUT COOKIES

2 C brown sugar
1 C melted butter
2 eggs (well beaten)
1 C wheaties
1 C oatmeal

2 C flour
1 tsp baking powder
1 tsp soda
1 C salted peanuts
   (whole)

Cream shortening and sugar. Add well beaten eggs. Next, add sifted flour, baking powder and soda. Then add the oatmeal, wheaties and salted peanuts.

*This is a hearty cookie. The "bread and butter stick-to-the-ribs type". This goes better in the winter.*

## SOFT GINGER COOKIES

1 C brown sugar
3/4 C shortening
1 C sour cream
1 C molasses
1/2 tsp - each nutmeg,
   all-spice, cloves and
   cinnamon

2 tsp ginger
1/2 tsp soda
1 tsp baking powder
   (heaping)
1/2 tsp salt
flour to make soft dough

ICING
1 C sugar
1 egg white (beaten)

4 Tbsp boiling water
flavoring

Boil.

*Note: Since baking time is not included this recipe shouldn't be tried by a new bride.*

## SUGAR COOKIES

3 C flour
1 tsp baking powder
1/2 tsp salt
1 1/4 C sugar

1 C shortening
3 eggs
1 tsp vanilla
1 tsp lemon extract

Sift dry ingredients. Add shortening, beaten eggs, vanilla and lemon flavoring. Cool in refrigerator. Roll out and cut with cookie cutter. Bake on greased cookie sheet for 10 minutes at 375 degrees.

*These cookies make as good a dunker as a lard doughnut.*

## SOUR CREAM SUGAR COOKIES

| | |
|---|---|
| 3/4 C sugar | 1/2 Tbsp baking powder |
| 1/3 C shortening | 1 egg |
| 1 1/4 C flour | 1/4 tsp salt |
| 1/2 tsp soda | grated rind of 1 orange |

Blend sugar and shortening. Add beaten egg, salt and orange rind. Add flour which has been sifted with the soda and baking powder. Roll out thin and cut with cookie cutter and bake on greased cookie sheet for 10 minutes at 375 degrees.

*If you don't have oranges in the house, just skip the orange rind the recipe calls for - people aren't usually too fussy at lunch between the 9 and 11.*

## DREAM BARS

| | |
|---|---|
| 1/2 C butter | 1 C flour |
| 1/2 C brown sugar | |

Mix with finger tips and press mixture into 8" x 13" pan. Bake 10 to 12 minutes. Remove from oven. Spread following mixture on top of above:

| | |
|---|---|
| 2 eggs | 1/2 C coconut |
| 1 C brown sugar | 1 C nut meats |
| 1/2 tsp salt | 1 tsp vanilla |
| 2 Tbsp flour | |

Return to oven and bake about 20 minutes. Cut into squares.

*If you've been in the barn, wash your hands before you bake these because this recipe calls for mixing the ingredients with your fingertips.*

## HONEY DATE BARS

| | |
|---|---|
| 1 C honey | 1 lb chopped dates |
| 2 eggs | 1 C chopped nuts |
| 1 1/3 C flour | |

127

Beat the eggs and add honey, flour and baking powder. Beat well. Add vanilla, nuts and dates. Spread on cookie sheet 10 x 15 inches, one-fourth inch deep. and when baked cut in strips one-half inch wide and three inches long. Roll in powdered sugar before serving. Bake at 375 degrees for 12 minutes.

*Take heed about eating this bar if you wear plates. Some cooks get a little carried away with the dates, and these bars become a little bit too chewy!*

## DOUGHNUTS

| | |
|---|---|
| 1 C sugar | 1 C sour milk |
| 4 Tbsp melted lard | 1/2 tsp salt |
| 2 eggs | 1 tsp soda |
| 1 tsp cinnamon | 3 C flour |
| 1/2 tsp nutmeg | |

Combine the sugar, butter, beaten eggs and salt. Add sour milk to which soda has been added. Mix in the flour thoroughly. Roll out to about one-third inch thickness and cut with the doughnut cutter. Fry in deep fat till golden brown.

*Good for dunking. Lard doughnuts are as Lutheran as apple pie is American.*

## WATKINS COCOA FROSTING

| | |
|---|---|
| 1 C confectioners' sugar | pinch salt |
| 2 heaping Tbsp Watkins Cocoa | Watkins hot coffee to |
| 1/4 tsp Watkins Vanilla | blend |

Mix Watkins Cocoa, sugar, salt, add enough Watkins Coffee to make smooth paste. Add Watkins Vanilla, beat well. Put in bowl and they can frost their own doughnuts if they want to.

# FUNERAL AND
# OTHER DEAD SPREADS

# FUNERAL SPREADS

### BOLOGNA FILLING

1 1/2 C. ground bologna
2 hard boiled eggs finely
   chopped

4 Tbsp. salad dressing
1/2 tsp. salt
a little bit of pepper

*Smash together and put on bread or buns. Don't be stingy with Bologna Spread.*

### BRAUNSCHWEIGER FILLING

1/2 lb braunschweiger liver sausage
1/2 C. drained pickle relish
4-6 Tbsp salad dressing

Mix it all up and put on bread.

*Not a favorite of children, but then they either ate it or went hungry. Missouri Synods felt welcome in the "other" Lutheran churches when this was served.*

### CHEESE SPREAD

2 hard cooked eggs (grated)
1 sm jar pimento chopped
1/2 lb grated American Cheese

1 Tbsp chopped onion
salt and pepper

A spread used on rye or wheat bread and a favorite for funerals when serving light and dark sandwiches.

*Nice when different races will be present.*

## FUNERAL MEAT

A sandwich filling always used for lunches at funerals (used on buns or bread).

3 lbs minced ham (ground)
*Today it is known as bologna meat.*

12 eggs (hard boiled)                                1 pt sandwich spread
                                                     (Kraft)

Grind meat and hard boiled eggs. Mix in the pint of sandwich spread. Enough for 1 dozen buns.


## *HAM OR SPAM, THE KING OF ALL SPREADS*

### HAM AND EGG SANDWICH

3 hard boiled eggs chopped
1 C baked or boiled ground ham or spam
3/4 C homemade mixed pickle relish
3/4 C mayonnaise
1 tsp chopped onion (if desired)

Mix together thoroughly and spread generously between slices of bread or opened faces. Also works well on open faced buns.


### INGEBRIT'S EGG SANDWICH SPREAD

2 hard cooked eggs                                   1/2 tsp salt
1 sm onion (minced)                                  3 pimentos
1/2 lb American cheese

Chop the eggs; dice pimentos and cheese; add onions and salt and pepper. Put together with this dressing;

1 Tbsp butter                                        3 Tbsp vinegar
1 Tbsp sugar                                         1/2 C milk

1 Tbsp flour

Mix and boil till clear.  Yields 2 cups.

*Ingebrit said to go easy on the onion if serving at a funeral where the mourners are getting up there in age when spices don't sit so well.*

## OTHER   SPREADS

### BASIC EGG SALAD FILLING

| | |
|---|---|
| 4 hard-cooked eggs, chopped fine | 1/2 tsp prepared mustard |
| 3 Tbsp chopped sweet pickle | 1/4 tsp onion salt |
| 3 Tbsp salad dressing | few grains pepper |

*This one gets the vote from the woman who needed a quick sandwich spread to serve a Luther League. It was usually served on wheat or white, or if you really want to jazz things up, you take one slice of white and one of wheat, put in the filling, cut the bread diagonally, and you would have yourself a two-toned sandwich.*

### LADIES AID SUPREME - DRIED BEEF ON WHITE

Butter white bread.  Put on one or two thin layers of dried beef and watch the sandwiches disappear.

### CHICKEN OR TURKEY FILLING

| | |
|---|---|
| 1 C minced cooked chicken | 3 Tbsp thick sour cream |
| 1/4 C finely chopped celery | 1/4 tsp salt |
| 1 tsp minced parsley | a little bit of pepper |

Mix this all together and put on buns.

*This was usually used for fancy occasions such as weddings, showers, or anniversaries.*

## DELUXE SPREAD

Spread rye bread with Cheeze Whiz. Lay the stuffed olives on side like watermelon and cut into cute little rings. Place on rye bread in pattern, and cut rye bread on the diagonal.

*Pretty as a picture and easy to eat.*

## NOVELTY SANDWICH SPREAD

American cheese on wheat
Thinly sliced radishes on homemade buttered whole wheat bread
Peanut butter and jelly
Summer sausage on white bread

*These are not necessarily served in a church but sometimes you see something like this.*

## SANDWICH SECRETS

1. Use bread one day old.

2. Let butter stand one hour at room temperature and cream thoroughly, do not melt butter.

3. Use plenty of filling and spread to edge.

4. For thin sandwiches, spread loaf with creamed butter; then slice. Butter each slice of bread.

5. Lettuce keeps sandwich moist. Have lettuce crisp.

6. Do not have fillings too moist or too dry.

7.   Toasted sandwiches should be spread with filling but no butter.  Spread outside with melted butter and toast in oven.

8.   The secret of good sandwiches is in having filling well seasoned.  Use Watkins Pepper, Watkins Celery Salt, Watkins Onion Seasoning, Watkins Dry Mustard and Watkins Paprika.

## FUNERAL PLATES

### GERMAN LUTHERAN FUNERAL PLATE

Bratwurst

Beans

Chips

Pickles

Cakes

Coffee

### SCANDINAVIAN LUTHERAN FUNERAL PLATE

Hotdish

Pickles

Cake

Coffee

# LUTEFISK SUPPERS

# LUTEFISK SUPPERS

## CHURCH BASEMENT LUTEFISK FEEDS

If there were ever justification for second helpings, it was at the annual church basement lutefisk feeds.  After reading the following list of foods needed for one of these huge undertakings, you will know why the red-armed, tired women who prepared this feast were hustled out of the kitchen for a heartful round of applause.

*Lutefisk dinner for 1200*
600 pounds of lutefisk
400 pounds of meatballs
116 pounds of butter
600 pounds of potatoes
276 cans of corn
40 gallons of cold slaw
40 quarts of dill pickles
20 quarts of beet pickles
600 pieces of lefse
20 loaves of rye bread (for the Swedes)
60 dozen buns
3,500 cups of coffee
Between 5,000-6,000 Scandinavian cookies such as krum-kaka, spritz, etc.

Vaer so god!!!

FOOTNOTE:  Our Scandinavian ancestors did not have the standard English measurements that we use today.  Their recipes may have called for all kinds of odd measures:

> barneskje - (child's spoon)
> teskje - (half a teaspoon)
> spiseskje - (one soup spoon)
> en smule - (a crumb of this or that)
> knap en liter - (not quite a liter)

# SALADS

## COLE SLAW DRESSING

10 Tbsp. sugar
1 tsp. dry mustard
1 tsp. salt
Beat the above together and add slowly:
1/2 C. vinegar
1/2 tsp. celery salt or celery seed and a trace of garlic.

1 C. oil
1 C. small onion, grated

## PICKLED BEETS

Wash beets thoroughly. Boil until tender. Remove skins and dice. To 5 quarts diced beets add 5 cups of liquid in which beets were boiled, 1 cup vinegar, 1 cup sugar and 5 tsp. salt. Bring to boil; pour over beets and seal. Heat before serving and drain off liquid and add butter. For Harvard Beets thicken the juice with a little cornstarch mixed with cold water and boil. Add vinegar and sugar to taste.

# FLATBREADS

## FLATBRØD

1 C. graham flour
2 C. white flour
1 tsp. salt

1 Tbsp. shortening
2 C. boiling water

Mix and let stand until cold. Add more flour and roll thin. Bake in oven on flat surface.

## KNÄCKEBRÖD II
### (Hard Tack)

1 C. coarse rye meal
1 C. rye flour
1 Tbsp sugar

1 1/2 tsp. salt
4 Tbsp. butter
1/2 C. milk

METHOD: Sift dry ingredients, cut in butter, add milk and stir until smooth. Turn onto floured board and roll very thin. Prick with fork, then cut dough into oblong pieces. Use a thimble and make holes in each piece. Place on slightly greased baking sheet and bake 10 minutes in a slow oven.

### KNAKE BROD (FLATBROD)

1 quart hot water; pour over 2 cups lard, 1/2 coup butter, 1 tsp. salt. Dissolve 2 cakes compressed yeast in 1/4 cup lukewarm water; add flour and yeast to warm water and shortening mixture. Knead well and let rise until double in bulk. Knead down and make small balls, let rest about 10 minutes. Roll out very thin, prick the surface with a fork and bake in a 400 degrees oven until brown on both sides. Cut into large squares and store in a dry place. This is a very large recipe.

### KNAKE BROD (FLATBROD)

2 cups flour, 4 tsp. baking powder, 1/2 cup shortening, 1/2 tsp. salt and 3/4 cup milk. Method: Mix shortening into dry ingredients, add milk. Roll out thin, put on cookie sheet, and prick with fork. Bake in 400 degrees oven until brown. This makes 12.

### RYE BREAD

| | |
|---|---|
| 1 C. milk | 1 C. water |
| 2 1/2 Tbsp. shortening | 1/2 C. molasses |
| 1/2 C. sugar | 1/2 tsp. ground anise |
| 1 tsp. salt | 2 pkgs. active dry yeast |
| 1 Tbsp. sugar | 1/4 C. warm water |
| 2 C. rye flour | 4 to 5 C. white flour |

Scald milk; add water, shortening, molasses, sugar, salt and anise. Dissolve yeast and 1 tablespoon sugar in 1/4 cup water. When milk mixture is lukewarm,add yeast, then rye flour, and mix until smooth. Add white flour until dough is easy to handle. Place in greased bowl and let rise until double. Divide into three balls. Cover and let rest 15 minutes. Form into loaves and place in well-greased tins. Let rise until double. Bake at 375° for 35 to 40 minutes. After removing from oven, brush with melted butter.

## LUTEFISK GRØT
### (Lutefisk Pudding)

| | |
|---|---|
| 1 C. rice | 1 tsp salt |
| 1 quart milk | 1 tsp sugar |
| 2 eggs, beaten | dash of nutmeg |
| 2 Tbsp. butter | cooked lutefisk |

METHOD: Scald rice, then cook in milk until thick. Add rest of ingredients and pour into a buttered baking dish. Add a little more scalded milk if necessary. Sprinkle with buttered bread crumbs and bake in moderate oven about 1 hour. This is a good way to use left over lutefisk. Other cooked fish such as pike, pickerel, salmon, etc. may also be used.

## LUTEFISK PUDDING

| | |
|---|---|
| 3/4 C. rice | 2 C. thin cream |
| 2 eggs | butter |
| 2 C. cooked lutefisk | salt and pepper to taste |

Cook rice in salted boiling water. Mix rice and lutefisk together; add cream, butter, salt and pepper. Bake in buttered baking dish, and serve with drawn butter. (A good way to serve left-over lutefisk).

## POTATO LEFSE

5 C. mashed potatoes
1 1/2 C. flour
2 Tbsp. melted butter
1 tsp. salt
1 tsp. sugar

Cook potatoes and mash the day before. Mash again before measuring. Makes 12 medium rounds.

## HARDANGER LEFSE

2 eggs                                              2 C. sour cream
1/2 tsp. soda                                       1/2 C. sugar
pinch of salt
1 1/2 tsp. ground cardamom (optional)
3 3/4 C. flour to roll

Put in refrigerator overnight. Go easy on flour as you can always
add more. Take a teaspoon and roll in flour like flatbread. Fry
on a pancake griddle a bit on both sides. Store in big container.
To serve, put between damp towels to moisten so they are soft.
Then spread with butter, sugar and cinnamon. Fold over and cut
in wedges to serve. A very old recipe.

## LEFSE

18 potatoes                                         1 tsp. salt
2 tsp. lard                                         flour

Boil and mash or rice potatoes. Cool. Add lard, salt and flour, a
little at the time until dough can be rolled out easily. Roll as
thin as possible. Bake on top of stove or on pancake griddle
until a light brown, turning frequently to prevent scorching. Use
moderate heat.

## LEFSE

5 large potatoes                                    3 Tbsp butter
1/2 C. sweet cream                                  1 tsp. salt
flour - Use 1/2 cup flour to each cup of mashed potatoes.

METHOD: Boil potatoes, mash very fine and add cream, butter
and salt; beat until light then let cool. Add flour and roll into
ball of dough, kneading until smooth. Form into a long roll and
slice in pieces about the size of a large egg, or larger, depending
on the size of lefse desired. Roll each piece round as for pie crust
and as thin as possible. Bake on lefse griddle or pancake griddle
until light brown, turning frequently so as not to scorch. Use
moderate heat. Do not grease the pan. When baked, place
between clean cloths or wax paper to keep them from becoming

dry. Serve cold with butter, sugar and cinnamon. Cut each lefse in half or fourths and roll up before serving.

## LEFSE

4 large potatoes, boil and mash; add 4 Tbsp. shortening, 6 Tbsp. cream. While still hot, add flour to make a dough that can be rolled out thin. Chill. Bake on pancake griddle until brown on both sides. Use spatula for turning pieces. Makes 12.

## LEFSE

| | |
|---|---|
| 4 C. riced potatoes | 1 tsp. salt |
| 1/4 C. shortening | 1 1/4 C flour |
| 1/4 C. very rich cream (creamery) | |

Cook potatoes and rice while hot. Add salt, shortening, and cream. Cool. Just before you roll your lefse, add the flour. A pastry cloth and sleeve work well when you roll it out. Makes 10 to 12.

## LUTEFISK

Soak lutefisk in cold water for 3-4 hours before using. Remove dark skin and fins, and cut in serving size pieces. Place in cheese cloth and put on to boil in a kettle of cold water, to which salt has been added. Cook about 5 minutes until fish is tender, then drain and serve with drawn butter or a cream sauce.

VARIATION: Try a little prepared mustard with lutefisk and butter.

## LUTEFISK

Cut off head and tail from fish and then cut fish into 4-inch lengths. Soak in mild saltwater over night. In the morning, soak in clear, cold water for 5 hours. Drain well. Put fish into cheesecloth bags or sugar sacks, filling bags half full. Drop fish bags into boiling, salted water and boil for five minutes. Remove bags from water and drain. Skin and bone fish with a spoon. Keep fish warm in a large bowl or crock until ready to serve. Serve with melted butter.

## WHITE SAUCE FOR LUTEFISK

2 Tbsp. butter                   1 C. milk
2 Tbsp. flour                   dash of pepper
1/4 tsp. salt

METHOD: Make a white sauce and add seasonings to taste. For variation, add a teaspoon of prepared mustard to sauce.

## MEATBALLS

For meatballs, mince two pounds of round,
Then add a pound of porksteak, ground.
A cup of "taters, then you mash
And beat two eggs into this hash.
One cup of breadcrumbs, all dried up.
Some fresh sweet milk, about a cup.
Two teaspoons use to salt it down,
And one of sugar - best if brown.
Half teaspoons each of ginger, cloves,
And allspice in the mix now goes;
Nutmeg and pepper add to taste,
Then stir till mixture is a paste.
Now form in balls, and roll in flour,
And fry them well for half an hour.
Add cream, one pint, then let them bake,
Which forty minutes more will take.

## SWEDISH MEATBALLS

4 lb. ground beef           2 lb. lean pork
3 beaten eggs              2 C. dry bread crumbs
2 C. cold water or milk if    3 tsp. salt (1 tsp to
    you prefer                  1 lb. meat)
1/2 tsp. allspice           1 tsp. pepper
1/4 C. onion

Makes balls of about 40.

*This recipe was used for lutefisk suppers and smorgasbords. It was Nettie Sathers recipe from Hauges.*

## KJØTKAKER (NORWEGIAN MEATBALLS)

2 1/2 lbs. ground round steak     1/2 onion
1/2 C. suet     1 tsp. baking powder
2 1/2 tsp. salt     1 C. cream
1/4 tsp. pepper     1 egg
1/8 tsp. nutmeg

Grind meat and suet very fine, beat egg slightly. Boil and cool cream. Mince onion fine. Add egg, cream, onion, seasonings and baking powder to meat and beat thoroughly until very light. Form into small balls, brown in butter and steam in gravy.

## KOTTBOLLAR (SWEDISH MEATBALLS)

3 lbs. ground beef     2 tsp. salt
1 quart cream     1/4 tsp. pepper
1 C. bread crumbs     1/4 tsp. allspice

Grind beef very find, add cream and beat thoroughly. Add seasonings and bread crumbs. (Rice Krispies or corn flakes, crushed fine, may be substituted for bread crumbs). Mix with beater until light. Form into small balls, brown in butter and make gravy from drippings, and simmer meatballs therein.

## SWEDISH MEATBALLS IN GRAVY

10 slices white bread     3 tsp. salt
1/2 tsp. white pepper     4 eggs
1/2 tsp. nutmeg     2 Tbsp. lemon juice
1/2 C. minced onion     1/2 tsp. paprika
1 tsp. Worcestershire sauce     1/4 C. chopped parsley
3 lbs. meat, ground

Soak bread in water to cover; squeeze out. Add beaten eggs to bread and remaining ingredients. Mix thoroughly with fingers. Form into 32 balls about 1 1/2 inch in diameter; do not press hard. Roll in seasoned flour. Brown balls on all sides in 1/2 cup hot fat in dutch oven. Mix 1/2 cup flour with 1 cup chicken stock or bouillon and add 3 cups more liquid and pour over meat balls. Reduce heat and simmer 50 minutes. If gravy is too thin, thicken with small amount of flour and water. Serves 16.

## POTATOES

Some Boil
Some Mash
Some Rice
But only russets will suffice!

## COOKIES AND GOODIES
## SWEET SOUP AND GRØT

### BERLINER KRANSE

| | |
|---|---|
| 2 raw egg yolks (beat) | 1 C. butter |
| 1 hard boiled egg yolk | 1/2 C. sugar |
| 3 C. flour | |

Mash boiled yolk with the sugar. Add the rest of ingredients. Roll with fingers to pencil size. Loop. Dip in beaten egg whites and then in sugar - preferably crushed loaf sugar. Bake at 350° until slightly browned.

### FATTIGMAND

| | |
|---|---|
| 12 egg yolks | 1 C. whipping cream |
| 1/2 C. sugar | 3 3/4 C. flour |

Beat egg yolks alone for 20 minutes; then with sugar for 15 minutes. Add cream, whipped, and flour a little at a time, leaving some of the flour for rolling. Let stand overnight in a cool place, roll out and bake in deep fat.

### KLEINER-FATTIGMAND (DANISH)

| | |
|---|---|
| 1 C. sugar | 1 tsp. vanilla |
| 1/2 C. butter | 1 tsp. baking powder |

147

2 eggs  
6 tablespoons sweet cream

flour enough to make a  
soft dough

Roll 1/4 inch thick, cut in strips 1 1/2 by four inches. Cut slit in each and put end through to form a twist. Fry in deep fat till light brown.

## KRINGLE

1 C. sugar  
1 C. sweet cream  
1 C. buttermilk  
6 C. flour

1 tsp. soda  
1 tsp. baking powder  
1/4 tsp. nutmeg

Sift flour, soda, baking powder and nutmeg together. Add sugar, cream and buttermilk gradually, mixing well. Roll out on floured board or cloth, cut into 1/4 inch strips about 4 inches long. Form into kringle and bake on oiled cookie sheet for 20 minutes at 375°.

## KRINGLER (DANISH)

4 C. flour  
1 C. butter  
1/2 C. sugar

2 C. sour cream  
1/4 tsp. salt  
1 tsp. soda

Sift together flour, sugar, salt and soda. Cut butter into dry ingredients like pastry. Add cream and flour to make a soft dough to roll. Cut in strips 1/2 inch wide and 9 inches long. Form a figure 8. Dip in beaten egg white and sprinkle with sugar and bake at 400 degrees.

## KRUMKAKER

NORWEGIAN:  
1 egg  
1 kopp suker  
1 kopp hvetemel  
1 kopp potetmel  
1 kopp smør  
1 kopp vann

ENGLISH:  
1 egg  
1 C. sugar  
1 C. wheat flour  
1 C. potato flour  
1 C. butter  
1 C. water

Mix well. Mixture is of consistency of light pancake dough. Heat iron. Experiment with heat until you find the correct temperature for your iron. Place about a soupspoonful of the mixture on the hot iron. Bake about 1/2 minute on that side. Turn the iron over and bake other side about 1/2 minute. A spatula is helpful in removing it. Roll cylinder. When slightly cool, remove it.

## KRUMKAKER

| | |
|---|---|
| 6 eggs | 1 C. butter |
| 1 C. sugar | 2 C. flour |

Beat eggs until light, adding sugar gradually. Add melted butter and flour a little at a time. Bake on iron and roll quickly; or form into patty shells, fill with fruit and top with whipped cream.

## MOUSIES OR SNOWBALLS

| | |
|---|---|
| 1 C. butter | 1/4 tsp salt |
| 1/2 C. confectioners sugar | 1 tsp vanilla |
| 2 1/4 C sifted flour | 3/4 C. finally chopped nuts |

Mix in order given and form into small balls. Bake at 400 degrees for 15 minutes. While still hot roll in powdered sugar. Let cool and roll in powdered sugar again.

## NORWEGIAN BUTTER COOKIES

| | |
|---|---|
| 3/4 C. butter | 1 tsp. vanilla |
| 1/2 C. sugar | 1 C. flour |
| 1 egg | 3/4 C. cornstarch |
| 1 tsp. baking powder | |

Melt butter and cool until lukewarm, add sugar and beat well. Add well beaten egg, vanilla and dry ingredients sifted together. Drop by spoonfuls 2 or 3 inches apart. Bake 16 to 18 minutes at 350°.

## B. G. ROSETTES

| | |
|---|---|
| 2 eggs (well beaten) | 1 C. milk |

1 tsp. sugar                    1 C. flour
1/4 tsp. salt

Heat lard or other cooking fat to 375 degrees. Let rosette iron
heat in fat before dipping into dough. Shake off excess fat.
When you dip iron into dough be very careful to avoid getting
dough on top of iron. If dough does not adhere to iron, the iron
may be too cold or have too much fat on it.

Bake in hot fat, 375°, until light brown. Ease rosette off iron
onto an absorbent towel. Makes about 40.

## ROSETTES

1 C. flour                     2 eggs
1 C. sweet milk                1 tsp. sugar

Beat eggs lightly, add sugar, milk and flour, mixing until
smooth. Fry in deep fat on rosette iron, cooling the iron each
time while sugaring the rosette just baked. Having the iron too
warm makes the rosettes greasy.

## SANDBAKKELSE

1 C. butter                    1 egg
1 C. sugar                     1/2 C. finely chopped
2 C. flour                         blanched almonds

Cream butter and sugar, add flour a little at a time. Add egg and
almonds. Press into tins and bake, oven temperature 350 degrees.

## SPRITS

1 C. brown sugar               1/2 tsp. cream of tartar
1/2 C. butter                  2 C. flour
1 egg                          1 tsp. ginger
1 tsp soda                     1 tsp. lemon extract

Cream butter, add sugar gradually, well beaten egg, soda dissolved in warm water. Add flour, cream of tartar and ginger, sifted together; lemon extract last. Put through cookie press.

## SPRUTBAKKELSE

1/2 C. butter
1/2 c. Crisco
1 C. sugar
1 egg, beaten

1/2 tsp. salt
1 tsp. vanilla
about 2 cups flour

Cream shortening, add sugar gradually, beaten egg and vanilla. Add flour and salt, mixing well. Put dough in cookie press and make cookies of various designs.

## STRULL

3/4 C. sugar
1 1/2 C. flour
1 C. whipping cream

1/2 C. half and half
1/2 C. whole milk
ground cardamon

Mix sugar and flour well and add the cardamon. Add one cup whipping cream and stir until smooth. Add the half and half and the whole milk. Bake on heated strull iron on both sides until light brown. Roll on cone while hot. Makes about four dozen.

## ROME GROT

1 C. butter (melted)
1 C. buttermilk (cold)

1 C. flour (mix smooth)

Bring to a boil.

3 C. cold milk

Salt (small amount)

## ROMME GROT (Scandinavian)

1 quart whipping cream (at least
    24 hours old)
1 Tbsp. sugar
1 quart milk (boiled)

1 tsp. salt

1 C. flour

Use heavy kettle, boil cream 10 to 15 minutes. Add flour slowly using a wire whip to keep mixture smooth, keep boiling on lower heat and stirring until butter appears. Add boiled milk and boil and stir to right consistency. Add sugar and salt. Put into bowl and pour butter over. Sprinkle with sugar and cinnamon. Serve lukewarm.

### RISENGREN (Rice Soup)

Cook rice. Add rich milk to make it soupy and a cinnamon stick. Cook slowly for an hour stirring frequently. Serve with sugar.

### SØTSUPPE (Sweet Soup)

| | |
|---|---|
| 2 quarts water | 2 sticks cinnamon |
| 1/2 C. sago | 1 C. sugar |
| 1 C. raisins | 1 Tbsp. vinegar |
| 1 C. prunes | 1 glass jelly or grape juice |
| 1 lemon | |

Wash sago, raisins and prunes. Cook sago, raisins and prunes in water for an hour. Add sugar, cinnamon, sliced lemon and vinegar. Boil again for thirty minutes; add jelly or grape juice about fifteen minutes before soup is cooked.

### SWEET SOUP

| | |
|---|---|
| 2 lbs. prunes | 1/2 C. currants |
| 1 lemon and peel | 1 1/2 C. raisins |
| 1 C. pearl tapioca or sago | 1 1/2 C. sugar |

Soak fruit overnight. Soak tapioca. Cook prunes, raisins and lemon. Add tapioca and cook over low heat until tiny spots inside "pearls" show. Add sugar and cinnamon or cinnamon sticks.

# HARVEST FESTIVALS

Ham was served, and blessings were counted. At the end of the meal the offering plate was passed, and we were challenged to "give until it hurts." Some did. Others ate their ham, put in their dollar, and went home.

# HARVEST FESTIVALS
## (Foods placed as usually remembered on table)

### HARVEST BEETS

| | |
|---|---|
| 1/4 C. sugar | 1-3 Tbsp corn starch |
| 1/4 C. weak vinegar | 1 tsp. butter |
| 1 C. diced beets (cooked) | |

Mix sugar and corn starch; add the vinegar. Boil for 5 minutes. Pour over the diced beets; allow to stand over slow flame for about 15 to 20 minutes. Add butter before serving.

### BUNS

Soak 2 cakes compressed yeast in 1 cup cold water. In a large bowl, put 1 cup hot water, 1 cup shortening, 1/2 cup sugar. When cool, add yeast and water, 1 1/4 tsps. salt, 2 beaten eggs, 6 1/2 cups flour. (Do not sift flour before measuring). Let rise, knead down and let rise again; then form into buns. Makes 48 buns.

### HAM, PINEAPPLE AND SWEET POTATO

| | |
|---|---|
| 1 1-inch slice ham | 1/4 tsp. cloves |
| 1 No. 2 can sliced pineapple | 1/4 tsp mustard |
| 3 sweet potatoes | 2 Tbsp. brown sugar |

Place ham in pan; sprinkle with cloves, mustard, and brown sugar. Cover with slices of pineapple. Cut sweet potatoes lengthwise, which have been cooked and peeled. Dip in fat and place around ham. Cover with pineapple juice to the depth of one-half inch and bake for 25 minutes at 375°.

### SCALLOPED HAM AND POTATOES

| | |
|---|---|
| 2 1/2-inch thick slices of | pepper |
| smoked ham | celery salt |
| 4 C. sliced raw potatoes | mustard |
| salt | 2 C. milk |

155

Lay one slice ham in bottom of casserole. Cover with thinly sliced potatoes. Season with salt, pepper, celery salt and mustard. Lay second slice of ham on top. Pour milk over all. (If necessary, use more milk to completely cover.) Sprinkle with bread crumbs, dot with butter, and bake at 375° for 1 hour.

## CARROT AND APPLE CASSEROLE

| | |
|---|---|
| 3 C. carrots, cooked and sliced | 1/2 C. brown sugar |
| 1 1/2 C. tart apples, sliced | 1/2 tsp. salt |
| 3 Tbsp. butter | 1/3 C. water |

Put a layer of carrots in a greased casserole and sprinkle lightly with salt. Cover this with a layer of apples, sprinkled with sugar and dotted with butter. Repeat until carrots and apples are used up. Add the water. Cover closely and bake in hot oven till apples are tender, then remove cover and allow to brown. Bake for 40 minutes at 375°.

## ENGLISH RAISIN CAKE

| | |
|---|---|
| 1 lb raisins | 2 tsp. soda |
| 1 1/2 C. sugar | 3 tsp. cinnamon |
| 1/2 C. butter | 1 tsp. nutmeg |
| 2 eggs | 1/8 lb. citron |
| 3 C. flour | 1/2 C. chopped nuts |

Simmer raisins in water to cover, using one cup of water there from in cake. Cream sugar and butter. Add eggs, beating well. Add sifted dry ingredients alternately with the water. Add fruit and nuts. Mix thoroughly. Bake for 45 minutes at 375° in a 9x14 inch pan.

## MAPLE NUT CAKE

| | |
|---|---|
| 1/3 C. shortening | 3/4 C. milk |
| 2 tsp. baking powder | 1 C. light brown sugar |
| 1 1/2 C. flour | 1 C. nuts |
| 2 eggs | 1/2 tsp. salt |
| 1 tsp. vanilla | |

Cream shortening with brown sugar. Add egg yolks. Mix and add milk. Sift and add flour, salt and baking powder. Add nuts and vanilla. Fold in beaten egg whites. Bake 35 minutes at 325 degrees.

## WATKINS ECONOMY SPICE CAKE
### *(Butterless, Eggless and Milkless)*

1 C. brown sugar
1 C. boiling water
1 C. raisins (more if desired)
1/3 C. lard
1/4 tsp. Watkins Nutmeg
1 tsp. Watkins Cinnamon
1 1/2 C. flour

1/8 tsp. Watkins Cloves
1/4 tsp. Watkins Ginger
1/4 tsp. Watkins Allspice
1/2 tsp. salt
1 1/2 tsp. Watkins
   Baking Powder
1 1/2 tsp Watkins Vanilla

Boil sugar, water, lard, raisins together about 3 minutes until sugar is well dissolved. Put aside until cold. Sift flour, Watkins Baking Powder, and spices together. Add to above mixture, then add flavoring. Bake in moderate oven. Use small square tin.

# MISSION FESTIVALS

# MISSION FESTIVALS

## BLOOD BOLOGNA

2 C. blood
3 grated raw potatoes
1/2 tsp. soda
1/2 tsp. pepper
3 Tbsp salt
1 Tbsp. allspice
2 C. leaf fat (cut up in cubes)

2 C. sour milk or
  buttermilk
2 C. sweet milk can be
  used instead of
  buttermilk and soda
3 C. white flour to 1 C.
  graham

Mix liquid, adding potato, sifting in dry ingredients. Stir in fat. Have sacks of muslin sewed 3x8 inches, filled 3/4 full and tied well. Place in boiling water, cook 2 hours. If sweetening is desired, add some raisins or little brown sugar.

## COVERED WAGON COOKIES

2 qt. sorghum
1 pt. corn syrup
4 C. sugar
1 Tbsp. allspice
1 1/2 tsp. cloves
about 24 C. flour (in all)

5 qt. black walnuts or 2 qt.
  walnuts and the rest
  pecans
4 Tbsp. soda (dissolved in
  1/4 C. warm water)
1 C sour cream

These cookies came with my grandmother on a covered wagon when she left Ladysmith, Wisconsin, to settle in Spring Valley. One batch makes a bushel of cookies and the older they get the better they are. That is why they are called covered wagon cookies, as they came with many a wagon across the prairies. The longer they are keep the chewier they become and the more flavorful.

Mix in a dishpan the sofghum, corn syrup and sugar. Cook these ingredients just to dissolve the sugar. Add 1 tablespoon of salt dissolved in a little water to this. Add 4 cups flour to this and place in a cool place, not the refrigerator.

The day before you want to start baking, set the pan in a warm place. Add cinnamon, allspice, cloves, walnuts and sour cream. Dissolve the 4 tablespoons soda in 1/4 C. warm water and add to mixture. Knead well and gradually put in more flour. In all, this takes about 24 cups of flour. Four you have already mixed. See that 20 more cups get mixed in, including the cup or two that you might use when you roll them out. Roll at least 1/4 inch thick and cut about 1 inch wide and 3 inches long. You can cut shapes, but there are so many you may wish to just use the bars. Bake each bar separately however, not as bar cookies. 8 minutes at 350°. Store in tight tin cans; don't freeze.

These are not sweet cookies. You can glaze them if you wish with 1 cup sugar, 1 cup water cooked and cooled. We kept them from Thanksgiving to Thanksgiving.

## DEVILED EGGS

6 hard boiled eggs                1/2 tsp dry mustard
1/8 tsp pepper                    1/2 tsp salt
about 3 Tbsp salad dressing or cream

After you cut the hardboiled eggs in halves, scoop out yolks and mash the devil out of them. Stir in the rest of the ingredients and fill the hollowed out eggs with the egg yolk mixture.

*A good thing to bring to a missionary picnic when time and money is a little tight. Fancy it up with a dash of paprika.*

## EASY HOT DISH

1 1/2 C. raw cubed potatoes       1 1/2 C. cubed raw coarse
1 can of Cream of Celery soup        balony (Fancy people
                                     spell it bologna)

Mix and cover. Bake at 350° for 45 minutes. The last minutes put on strips of cheese. Serves 2.

*Only someone who didn't have kids would think of making a casserole that served only two.*

## HAMBURGER HOT DISH

Brown 1 lb. hamburger with 1 small onion. Mix with 1 can Cream of Mushroom Soup, 1 can of Cream of Chicken Soup and 1 can of cream style corn. Pour mixture over about 5 sliced potatoes in a large casserole. Bake 1 hour at 350 degrees.

*Mrs Benson said, "If you don't cook this long enough, it gets kind of soupy and hard to eat if it's on a thin paper plate.*

## HAMBURGER RICE HOT DISH

Brown 1 lb. hamburger and 1 onion. Add 2 cans Chicken Gumbo, 1 can water and 1 cup raw rice. Bake in covered casserole for 1 1/2 hours at 350°. More liquid may be added if needed. Keep it covered.

*The late Mrs. Sven Hanson didn't keep it covered and her hamburger rice hot dishes were always dried out.*

## HOT DISH

| | |
|---|---|
| 2 lbs ground veal or beef | 1 C. diced celery |
| 1 lb. ground salt pork | 1 C. diced carrots |
| 1 C. bread crumbs | 1 onion, diced |
| 2 eggs | 1 can tomato soup |
| 2 Tbsp fat | 1 can water |

Mix ground meat, salt pork, bread crumbs and slightly beaten eggs. Form into meat balls and brown in the fat. Put in a baking dish. Mix celery, carrots, onion, tomato soup and water, and pour over the meat balls. Bake for 1 hour at 325 degrees. This serves 10.

*Most people wouldn't use veal at a Lutheran Church festival. Hamburger is sufficient.*

## HOT DISH FOR 100

| | |
|---|---|
| 1/4 C. shortening | 3 No. 2 cans corn |
| 3 qts tomatoes | 5 lbs ground beef |
| 3 cans green beans | 50 averaged sized potatoes |

5 lbs. macaroni
3 bunches celery

30 med. onions, diced

Cook and drain macaroni. Brown meat and onion together. Dice potatoes and cook about 10 minutes. Some of the potato water may be saved to be used for moisture if needed. Mix all together and bake. Carrots may be added if desired or if you have to stretch it.

*This is a good old stand by for funerals too. Especially funerals of members who are in good standing and well liked by most.*

## HUNGARIAN GOULASH

1 lb. hamburger
1 C. chopped celery
2 C. cooked rice
1 No. 1 can tomatoes

2 Tbsp fat
1 small onion, if desired
1 can kidney beans

Melt fat in frying pan. Add hamburger and fry until brown, add celery and cook until celery is done. Then add cooked rice and strained tomatoes. Add kidney beans last, add salt and pepper to taste. Pour in baking dish and bake about 20 minutes

*Most Lutheran Church Basement Women don't serve Hungarian Goulash because it calls for a mix of celery and kidney beans and things that just don't go together well. It would be like mixing a regular Lutheran with a Wisconsin synod German Lutheran.*

## EVERYDAY JELLO

1 small box jello
1 cup hot water
1 cup cold water

Dissolve jello in hot water. Add cold water and set. This recipe can be doubled.

*Most Lutheran Women would add 1 large banana and/or whipping cream for a Mission Festival. But then, some don't. Good for those with new dentures or those on special liquid diets.*

## MEXICAN GOULASH

| | |
|---|---|
| 1 lb. bacon | 1 box spaghetti or noodles |
| 1 can corn | 1 can tomatoes |
| 1 can lima beans | 1 can peas |

Prepare spaghetti or noodles according to directions on box. Fry the bacon and add it to the spaghetti also adding a little of the drippings. Then add corn, tomatoes, lima beans and peas, (drain the liquid from the beans and peas). Season to taste.

*A festive dish to bring if the missionaries are from the South of the border, even though most Midwest Lutherans don't care for this dish.*

## NUT DEVIL'S FOOD

| | |
|---|---|
| 2 1/3 C. sifted flour | 1/2 C. shortening |
| 3 tsp. baking powder | 2 C. sugar |
| 1/2 tsp. salt | 4 eggs |
| 2 squares chocolate | 1 tsp. vanilla |
| 1 C. milk | 1 C. chopped walnuts |

Sift flour, baking powder and salt together. Cream shortening thoroughly, add sugar gradually until light and fluffy. Add beaten yolks, mixing thoroughly, then melted chocolate, and beat well. Add sifted dry ingredients, alternately with milk, mixing well after each addition. Add flavoring and nuts. Fold in egg whites beaten stiff but not dry. Bake at 350 degrees. This makes 3 layers or a 9x12 loaf. Bake the layers for 30 minutes, the loaf for 50.

*If you are on a committee for the festival, you won't have enough time to make this.*

## OATMEAL CAKE

| | |
|---|---|
| 2 C. oatmeal | 3 C. brown sugar |
| 2 C. water (boiling) | 1 1/2 C. lard |

Pour boiling water over oatmeal. Add sugar and lard.

Combine:

2 C. bread flour  
1 tsp. soda  
1 tsp. salt  

2 tsp. cinnamon  
1 tsp. baking powder  
1 egg  

You may add as many raisins and nuts as you like. Bake in 10x13 inch pan at 350 degrees for 45 minutes. Serve with whipped cream.

*This is kind of a bother for mission festivals. Mrs. Peder Larson said, "Skip the whipped cream for pot luck tables. It's tasty without it.*

## PREACHER'S HOT DISH

1 lb. hamburger  
2 medium onions or less  
2 C. celery  
1 can tomato soup  
1 can mushroom soup  

1 1/4 C. water  
2 C. chow mein noodles  
1 tsp. chili powder  
salt and pepper to taste  

Brown hamburger, onions and celery in small amount of fat. Add remaining ingredients except noodles. Add noodles and mix well. Sprinkle top with additional noodles before baking. Bake at 350 degrees.

*We don't know why this is called a Preacher's Hot Dish. Maybe its because the chow mein noodles add a bit more class.*

## RHUBARB SAUCE

4 C. diced rhubarb  

1 C. brown sugar  

Small amount of water in bottom of kettle.

Put rhubarb, sugar, and water in kettle and cook until tender. This is always a good dessert in the spring and early summer.

*If you are busy or don't have time to bake or cook for a mission festival, you always have a jar of rhubarb sauce on hand to bring.*

## SALMON HOT DISH

1 tall can salmon
1 No. 2 can peas
1 C. shell macaroni
3 hard cooked eggs

1/2 C. breakfast cereal
   flakes
1/2 tsp. salt
1/8 tsp. pepper

Boil macaroni in water, to which 1/4 teaspoon salt has been added, for five minutes. Drain. Mix salmon (flaked), peas, diced eggs, salt, pepper and macaroni. Make a white sauce, using juice from salmon for part of the liquid. Pour over other ingredients and mix well. Top with crushed cereal flakes. Bake at 325 degrees for 30 minutes. Serves 6.

*A tall can of salmon can get kind of spendy, but if you don't' have any meat thawed, then you're up a creek without a paddle and might not have any other choice.*

## SPICE CAKE

1 1/2 C. brown sugar
2 eggs
1 tsp soda (in milk)
1 tsp. ground cinnamon
1/2 tsp. ground cloves

1/2 C. butter
1 C. sour milk
1 tsp. baking powder in 2
   cups flour

Just before putting in pan, add a tablespoon of vinegar.
1/2 C. chopped nuts may be added if desired.

*Make the usual frosting for this cake. Good in the Fall of the year.*

## STRING BEAN AND CARROT HOT DISH

2 Tbsp. butter
2 Tbsp. flour
1/2 tsp. salt
1/8 tsp. pepper
1 C. milk and vegetable juice

1/2 C. grated cheese
4 medium carrots cooked
4 eggs, hard cooked
2 C. string beans, cooked

In top of double boiler blend butter, flour, salt and pepper. Add the milk and stir until smooth. Melt the cheese in the hot sauce. Put carrots and eggs, both cut in halves lengthwise, in bottom of buttered baking dish. Place string beans around them. Pour cheese sauce over vegetables and bake at 375° for 30 minutes. Serves four.

*A good use for all those string beans you canned.*

## SYLTE
### (Head Cheese)

Clean pig's head thoroughly under running water. Place in cold salt water and boil until tender, about three hours. Leave in liquid until cool. Then remove meat from bones. Place a clean cloth in loaf pan. Cut meat into strips and arrange on cloth, alternating lean and fat meat. The rind of the meat should be placed so it will be on the outside of "sylte" roll. Season meat with salt, pepper and allspice to taste. Roll up cloth as tightly as possible to make "sylte" roll. Wrap string about roll and tie firmly. Place heavy weight on roll and press overnight. The cloth may then be removed and the head cheese will retain its shape. Place rolls in brine for 48 hours before using.

*Fit for King Olaf!*

## TATER - TOT HOT DISH

1 lb. hamburger, browned and seasoned with salt, pepper and onion
1 small can peas
1 can Cream of Mushroom Soup
1 can Cream of Celery Soup
1 pkg. frozen tater-tots

Put in layers in small casserole as listed. (When doubling the recipe, use only 3 cans of soup.) Bake at 350 degrees for 30-40 minutes. This will make a large cake pan full. It can be prepared the night before and baked the next day.

*A life saver for a busy Lutheran woman.*

# VEGETABLE HOT DISH

1 layer of raw potatoes
1 layer of raw onions
1 layer of raw ground meat
   (seasoned)

1 layer of cooked rice
1 layer of canned lima
   beans
1 can of tomatoes

Arrange layers of onions, potatoes, meat, rice, lima beans and season each layer as desired with salt and pepper. Pour tomatoes over layers and bake at 350° for 2 hours. Serves 6-8.

*This would be a Lutheran classic recipe if the lima beans and tomatoes weren't in it but rather Cream of Mushroom Soup.*

# BIBLE SCHOOL LUNCH BOX

## THE BIBLE SCHOOL LUNCH BOX

Lunches, whether for school children or grown-ups, should contain substantial food that will be wholesome, nourishing and appetizing. The Bible School lunch should be a real meal with enough variety to form a balanced diet.

A lunch should be packed in a well-ventilated, sanitary container to protect the food and to keep it compact and odorless on opening. Waxed paper should be used to wrap all food, and covered jelly glasses are excellent to use for baked beans, vegetable salad, applesauce, baked apple or for a pudding. Highly-seasoned and rich foods should not be placed in a lunch box. Plain, wholesome food is essential for health.

Milk in some form should be included in the daily Bible School lunch - either plain milk, malted milk, or hot or cold Watkins Cocoa, which may be carried in a pint milk bottle or in a thermos bottle, using a straw for drinking. Milk is highly important because it supplies energy and contains the necessary mineral salts, with Vitamins A, B, C, D and G. Milk contains calcium which quiets the nervous system. Fresh fruit in season is appetizing and healthful.

Hard cooked eggs, cooked 30 minutes, are as digestible as soft-boiled. Peeled, wrapped in a lettuce or cabbage leaf and waxed paper, they will make an appetizing salad. Cooked vegetables as a salad add a note of interest to a box lunch. Raw carrot sticks or celery sticks made crisp in cold water, dried and wrapped in waxed paper make a tasty accompaniment to a meat sandwich.

# SUNDAY SCHOOL PICNICS

# SUNDAY SCHOOL PICNICS

## JELLO FOR A CROWD

4 boxes Jello
4 C hot water
4 C cold water

Dissolve Jello in hot water. Be careful to get everything dissolved. Add cold water and refrigerate. When partially set, carefully slice in 1 good sized banana or 2 small. This will feed about 30 people. (This recipe was used for the 75th Anniversary of the Trinity Lutheran Church Sunday School Picnic. Add Banana for variation.)

## COMPANY CASSEROLE

1 1/2 lb. ground beef
2 medium onions
1 can mushrooms
1/2 C. stuffed green olives
1 box Juniorettes, cooked

1/2 C. grated American
  cheese
salt and pepper
1 can mushroom soup
1 C. milk, blended with
  soup

Brown ground beef and onions; add mushrooms and olives. Stir in cheese and seasonings, soup and Juniorettes. Mix a few cashews and chow mein noodles in with casserole. Bake at 350 degrees for 1/2 hour; remove from oven and sprinkle more noodles and cashews on top. Bake another 1/2 hour.

## MACARONI - SPAM BAKE

2 C. cooked macaroni
1 small onion
1 small green pepper (optional)
1/4 lb. cheese
1 can spam
pimento (optional)

1 1/2 C. hot milk
1/2 C. butter
1 1/2 C. bread crumbs
4 egg yolks, beaten
1 can mushroom soup
4 egg whites, beaten

Grind onions, pepper, cheese and spam. Melt butter in milk. Beat yolks of eggs; pour over bread crumbs. Add butter and milk. Fold in stiffly beaten egg whites. Mix gently with ground

177

ingredients. Bake in 9x13 inch pan. Cut in squares. Pour heated (undiluted) mushroom soup over each square when serving.

## FRIED CHICKEN FOR SUNDAY SCHOOL PICNICS

Preparation:   Go out to the chicken coop and find yourself about 14 old biddies who haven't been keeping up their end of the bargain as far as producing eggs goes.  Bring them to the chopping block and axe off their heads.  Let them flop around for awhile - half dead.  Whip them into the kitchen, and immerse them in scalding water to loosen the feathers.  Next, roll up a newspaper, set it on fire and singe the remaining feathers off.  (This is done after you lift them out of the boiling water).  Make sure you don't start anything else on fire!!  Take all the innards out, and you're ready to start.  (If you are planning to serve these chickens for a Sunday noon Sunday School picnic, it's best you do the preparation on Saturday so you're not rushed.)  Sunday morning - early a.m. - wash and cut up the 14 chickens.  Wipe them dry, season with a little salt and pepper, dip them in beaten eggs and flour, and fry them in hot lard on top of the stove. After they are done frying, put them in a big roaster and let them finishing baking while you are at church. When you get home from church, you can take the drippings and make a little gravy.

## TUNA CRUNCH SALAD

1 No. 1/2 can Star Kist Solid Tuna
4 1/2 Tbsp. chopped pickles
1 1/2 Tbsp. minced onion
1 C. mayonnaise
Dash of salt, if desired

1 1/2 Tbsp. lemon juice
1 1/2 C. shredded
   cabbage
1 small bag potato chips
   (coarsely crushed)

Combine tuna, pickles, onion, mayonnaise and lemon juice. Chill in covered dish until ready to serve.  Add cabbage and toss. Just before serving, add half of the crushed potato chips and toss lightly. Heap into shallow lettuce lines salad bowl, sprinkle with rest of chips.

## GRANDMA'S FAVORITE BAKED BEANS

For every cup of beans use 1 rounded tablespoon of brown sugar and 1 tablespoon molasses. Cover beans well with water and boil until hulls start to loosen. Add salt, sugar and molasses and 1 teaspoon dry mustard. Add bacon and a small onion and bake for at least 2 hours or more. 1 pound of beans = a roaster.

- Selma Nestegard

## POTATO SALAD FOR 100

Boil up 32 pounds of potatoes. Chill. Add 4 bunches of celery, 4 dozen hard boiled eggs, 8 green peppers, pickles, salad dressing, salt and pepper to taste. Recipe can be doubled for big crowds.

*A Sunday School Picnic MUST!!*

## REAL LEMONADE

Squeeze lemons
Add lemon pulp
Add sugar to taste
Put in ice cubes and chills.

## DESSERT

Dixie cups or ice cream cones are standard desserts at Sunday School picnics.

## LUTHER LEAGUERS AND
## WHAT THEY EAT

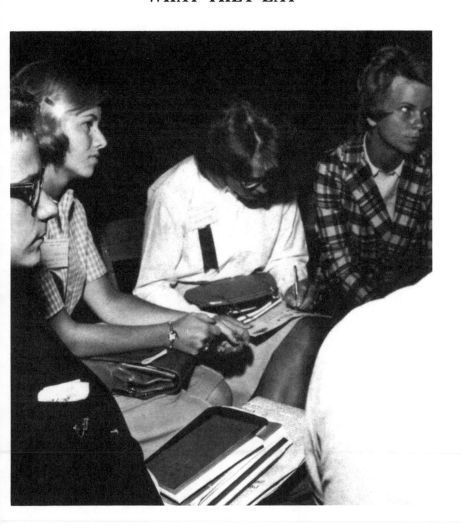

# LUTHER LEAGUERS AND
# WHAT THEY EAT

## BEVERAGES

### RED NECTAR DRINK
*Delicious, Refreshing Drink*

2 tsp Watkins Cherry
    Nectar Syrup

2 tsp sugar

Blend sugar and syrup in glass of water.

Stir the mixture and add an ice cube.

*Of course you'd have to make several pitchers of this red nectar drink for a thirsty bunch of Luther Leaguers, especially if there was a lot of boys at the meetings. Churches usually don't have ice cubes, but you can chill the nectar in the refrigerator while the meeting is on.*

### ICE CREAM SODA

3 Tbsp cocoa syrup
vanilla ice cream

1 Tbsp Watkins Vanilla
carbonated water (cold)
serve with siphon

Place syrup in tall glass. Add ice cream. Fill glass using one half carbonated water and one half milk. Stir to blend.

*A good treat for Luther Leaguers after they've done some volunteer work. Save for special occasions. It's usually not made for everyday.*

### WATKINS HOT COCOA

3 Tbsp Watkins Cocoa
2 Tbsp sugar
2 C milk

1 C boiling water
whipped cream
Watkins Vanilla
pinch of salt

183

Scald milk in double boiler, blend Watkins Cocoa, salt, sugar in a saucepan. Slowly stir in boiling water, boil 2 to 3 minutes. Stir cocoa mixture into hot milk. Cover, keep hot over boiling water. Just before serving, use rotary beater, whip briskly. Serve in hot cup with dash of whipped cream or marshmallow.

*Again, you'd have to make this in large quantities for Luther Leaguers. A dandy treat after a hayride!*

## MAIN DISHES

### BARBEQUES

10 lbs. hamburger                        salt and pepper
tomatoes and tomato soup

Brown the hamburger. Add tomatoes, tomato soup, and spices. Keep warm until you serve them in big buns.

### BEANIE WIENIES

8 frankfurters                        1 tsp salt
2 C cooked navy beans                 1/4 tsp pepper
1 can tomato soup, 10 1/2-oz.         1/4 tsp mustard
1 onion, sliced                       1 tsp worcestershire sauce

Split frankfurters lengthwise and cut each piece in half. Place a layer of cooked beans in buttered casserole, then half of the frankfurters and half the onion. Top with remaining beans, frankfurters and onion. Mix the soup with the salt, pepper, mustard and worcestershire sauce and pour over other ingredients. Cover and bake at 375° for 25 minutes.

*A wonderful treat after summer ball games.*

## CHILI CON CARNE

| | |
|---|---|
| 2 lbs. beef | 1 lge onion |
| 2 lbs pork | 2 No. 2 cans kidney beans |
| 3 Tbsp lard | 2 No. 2 cans tomatoes |
| 1 Tbsp chili powder | 1 tsp black pepper |
| 1 tsp salt | |

Dice meat; brown in lard.  Add the onion, cut in small pieces, and the other ingredients. Cook slowly for 2 hours.

*An international dish served by Lutheran Church Basement Women. This was never too spicy for the young who can handle chili powder.*


## LUTHER LEAGUE HOT DISH

| | |
|---|---|
| 1 C. boiled macaroni | 1 tsp salt |
| 1 1/2 C scalded milk | 3/8 tsp pepper |
| 1 C soft bread crumbs | 3/8 tsp paprika |
| 1 pimento, chopped | 1 1/2 C grated cheese |
| 1 tsp chopped parsley | 3 eggs |
| 1 Tbsp chopped onion | |

Pour scalded milk over bread crumbs.  Combine with the other ingredients, folding in well beaten eggs last.  Bake in a buttered casserole at 350 degrees for 50 minutes.  Most Luther Leaguers wouldn't fuss if you served them hot dish because they're used to it and learned at a young age not to complain.


## DESSERTS

### RICE KRISPIE BARS

| | |
|---|---|
| 1/4 C margarine or butter | 6 C. Rice Krispies |
| 1 pkg (10 oz.) marshmallows | |

(NOTE:  Use fresh marshmallows for best results)

Melt butter. Add marshmallows and melt. Add Rice Krispies. Press warm mixture into a 9x9x2 inch pan.

*These could be made and ready to serve Luther Leaguers in a wink of the eye.*

## BROWNIES

| | |
|---|---|
| 2 squares chocolate | 1/2 C butter |
| 2 eggs | 1 C sugar |
| 1/2 C flour | 1 tsp baking powder |
| 1 tsp vanilla | 1 C broken walnut meats |

Melt together the chocolate and butter. Beat together the eggs, sugar, flour and baking powder and then add to first mixture. Lastly stir in vanilla and nut meats. Pour on buttered paper in shallow pan and bake in moderate oven (300° to 350°) 20 to 30 minutes. Cut in bars.

*Brownies are to Luther Leaguers as apple pie is to America.*

# ABOUT THE AUTHORS

Janet Letnes Martin, daughter of the late John and Helen Klemetson Letnes, grew up in the rural setting of Hillsboro, North Dakota. Both her maternal and paternal grandparents came from Norway and helped settle this area. She received her B.A. form Augsburg College, Minneapolis, Minnesota, and furthered her studies at the University of Minnesota. In 1983 Janet wrote a family history book entitled *Reiste Til Amerika*. In 1984 and 1986, respectively, she co-authored *Cream and Bread* and *Second Helpings of Cream and Bread* with Allen Todnem of Hastings, Minnesota. In 1988, she wrote *Shirley Holmquist* and *Aunt Wilma; Who Dunit?* She and her husband, Neil Martin of Newfolden, Minnesota, reside in Hastings, Minnesota, with their three daughters, Jennifer, Sarah, and Katrina.

Allen Todnem, son of Kris and Cecelia Kallem Todnem, was born and raised in DeKalb, Illinois. His father immigrated to this country from Norway in 1926. Allen's maternal grandparents immigrated form Norway in the late 1800's and settled near Norway, Illinois. Allen attended Waldorf Jr. College, Forest City, Iowa, received his B.A. degree from Augsburg College, Minneapolis, Minnesota, and his M.A. from the University of Northern Iowa, Cedar Falls, Iowa. He is presently employed by the Hastings public school district as a senior high science teacher. In 1984 he co-authored a book with Janet Martin entitled *Cream and Bread*. And in 1986, they wrote *Second Helpings of Cream and Bread*. Allen and his wife, Patty Holmen of Windom, Minnesota, reside in Hastings, Minnesota, with their three children, Eric, Danny, and Suzanne.

# CREDITS FOR ILLUSTRATIONS

David Anderson Collection, NDIRS, NDSU, Fargo, *page 5.*

*Minnesota Historical Society*, families can vegetables, *page 27.*

*Minnesota Historical Society*, preparing lutefisk.   Photo: *St. Paul Daily News, page 137.*

# REORDER FORM
## FOR

## *LUTHERAN CHURCH BASEMENT WOMEN*

Name: _____

Address: _____

City: _____ State: _____ Zip: _____

No. of Copies_____ @ $9.95/copy   Subtotal_____

Postage & Handling $1.50 (per book)          _____

MN Residents add 6% Sales Tax                 _____

                                        Total   _____

Send cash, check, or money order to Redbird Productions, Box 363, Hastings, MN 55033.

If you have not read our other books, you must! You can order *Cream and Bread* or *Second Helpings of Cream and Bread* from Redbird Productions, Box 363, Hastings, MN 55033 for $7.95@ plus $1.50 shipping and handling.

If you wish to order *Shirley Holmquist & Aunt Wilma, Whodunit?* or receive a free copy of the MARTIN HOUSE HERALD, send $7.95 plus $1.50 for shipping and handling for the book to Martin House, Box 274, Hastings MN 55033.

If you wish to inquire about fundraiser prices for the books, or to order our Lutheran Church Basement Women dishtowels, send inquiries to Redbird Productions, Box 363, Hastings, MN 55033.

# REORDER FORM
# FOR

## *LUTHERAN CHURCH BASEMENT WOMEN*

Name: _____

Address: _____

City: _____ ·State: _____ Zip: _____

No. of Copies _____ @ $10.95/copy    Subtotal _____

Postage & Handling    $2.50 @ Book rate/copy    _____

$3.00 @ First class/copy    _____

(Maximum postage on multiple orders $10.00)    _____

MN Residents add 6.5 Sales Tax    _____

TOTAL    _____

Send cash, check, or money order to: Martin House, Box 274, Hastings, MN 55033, or call 1-800-950-6898.

If you are interested in our Lutheran Jell-o Power Apron, silk-screened dishtowel, or other books and products, call or write Martin House at the above address or phone number for a free copy of the Martin House Herald.

191